W9-CCB-354

The experts praise *Finding Keepers*

"Today's skilled employees are often more competent at selecting 'keeper' employers than companies are at selecting 'keeper' employees. Corporate America is demanding dramatically improved performance from marketing and HR professionals to insure companies get more than their fair share of the best talent. *Finding Keepers* is a great read for those who have talent acquisition as a critical part of their mission."

—Carl Camden, President & CEO, Kelly Services. Inc.

"The authors avoid the magic bullet approach with a systemic view of the problem. They dissect both attracting and retaining through a cogent explanation of effective processes. You have to read this one!"

—Dr. Jac Fitz-enz, author of *The ROI of Human Capital* and founder of the Saratoga Institute

"The authors have a bold goal . . . they want to completely reinvent the way you think about recruiting. Better to listen now, before it's too late."

—Seth Godin, author of *Meatball Sundae*

"The authors have nailed it! They give incredible advice on how to improve across the spectrum, from hiring great people to keeping them. If you're a recruiter or manager hoping to attract and retain top talent—even if you think you've seen it all—read *Finding Keepers* now!"

—Beverly Kaye and Sharon Jordan-Evans, coauthors of *Love 'Em or Lose 'Em: Getting Good People to Stay*

"Redefining the "Engagement Cycle," *Finding Keepers* highlights that effective recruiting and retention is much more than sorting résumés—it is good marketing. Pogorzelski, Harriott and Hardy, key Monster executives, stress the obvious world-wide skill shortage demands employers focus not only on their own needs but also the needs of the most desirable talent.

"Regardless of the employer's geography, industry or size, *Finding Keepers* offers many models and tools to help fit any employer's unique needs.

"With greater than forty million job seekers and as the first and continuing leader in its industry, the Monster experience is an exceptional source for the authors' unique insights."

—Michael R. Losey, SPHR, CAE, President,
MikeLosey.com, and President and CEO, Retired,
Society for Human Resource Management

"*Finding Keepers* is an essential guide to navigating today's complex global market for talent. The authors expertly summarize the challenges and then provide a practical blueprint for mastering them. I highly recommend this book."

—Allan Schweyer, Executive Director & President,
Human Capital Institute

Finding Keepers

The **Monster Guide** to **Hiring** and **Holding** the World's Best Employees

monster

Steve Pogorzelski and Jesse Harriott, Ph.D.
with Doug Hardy

Mc
Graw
Hill

New York   Chicago   San Francisco   Lisbon   London   Madrid   Mexico City
Milan   New Delhi   San Juan   Seoul   Singapore   Sydney   Toronto

Copyright ©2008 by Monster Worldwide LLC. All rights reserved. Printed in the United States of America. Except as permitted under the United States Copyright Act of 1976, no part of this publication may be reproduced or distributed in any form or by any means, or stored in a data base or retrieval system, without the prior written permission of the publisher.

1 2 3 4 5 6 7 8 9 0 DOC/DOC 0 9 8 7

ISBN: 978-0-07-149908-8
MHID: 0-07-149908-3

MONSTER, the Monster icon, and the Trumpasaurus character are registered trademarks of Monster Worldwide, Inc. and are used with its permission.

McGraw-Hill books are available at special quantity discounts to use as premiums and sales promotions, or for use in corporate training programs. For more information, please write to the Director of Special Sales, Professional Publishing, McGraw-Hill, Two Penn Plaza, New York, NY 10121-2298. Or contact your local bookstore.

Library of Congress Cataloging-in-Publication Data
Pogorzelski, Steve.
    Finding keepers / by Steve Pogorzelski and Jesse Harriott, with Doug Hardy.
      p. cm.
    Includes bibliographical references and index.
    ISBN 0-07-149908-3 (alk. paper)
    1. Employees—Recruiting. 2. Professional employees. 3. Employee retention. I. Harriott, Jesse. II. Hardy, Doug. III. Title.
HF5549.5.R44P64 2008
658.3'11—dc22

2007031758

This book is printed on acid-free paper.

Finding Keepers is dedicated to Monster employees worldwide, and to the following:

To Brenda, Sari, and Andrew for all of their support, inspiration, and love.

—S.P.

To my wife Evelyn, my son Jesse, and my daughter Eva— whose unconditional love and support inspire me each day.

—J.H.

This one is for Tommy and Jerry.

—D.H.

Contents

Introduction

If you want to know what kind of difference good hiring makes, invite a group of strangers to break your bones, dismantle your leg, and then reassemble the pieces while you sleep.

As we were writing this book, Steve Pogorzelski got a firsthand look what it means to have an exceptional group of talented people working together. It was December 2006, and he was scheduled to undergo hip surgery at New England Baptist Hospital (NEBH) in Boston.

The hospital is renowned for orthopedic surgery; its doctors perform 5,000 operations a year. It employs a lot of nurses, physical therapists, and administrators. People with those skills have their pick of workplaces in Boston, where you can't drive five blocks without seeing another renowned hospital. It's very hard to find and keep the best employees in a job market like that, but NEBH manages to do so by creating a unique workplace, not just for patients, but also for employees.

Steve recalls his experience at NEBH: "Before you do anything, you and your caregiver attend a two-hour informational class which includes physical therapy. Two weeks before surgery, you go to a preparation session. They tell you it's going to take an hour and a half. Everyone from the receptionist to the registrar dresses in a professional suit, as if they were working in a fine hotel. After quick paperwork, you walk to a room where a physical therapist, an occupational therapist, an anesthesiologist, and medical technicians are ready to see you. Except for the lab coats, you could still be in that fine hotel—professional demeanors, no delays. Everyone smiles and says, 'This way, Mr. Pogorzelski . . .'

They check your blood pressure, draw blood, and perform the usual prep work. One perfectly executed procedure seamlessly follows another, and you actually get out in an hour and a half. Later, you attend an advanced therapy class, it starts and ends on time, and you walk out thinking, 'that's the best two hours I could have spent before surgery.'

When was the last time you had a medical experience like that?

On its recruiting Web site, NEBH invites candidates to "look into the hospital everyone looks up to." Patients and visitors are referred to as customers. There's a formal "Dress to Impress" policy: "When you project a professional image, you have the power to make New England Baptist Hospital successful or not."

New England Baptist Hospital studied its practices and came up with a rare (for a hospital) understanding: by projecting a distinct attitude of customer service, they get better outcomes. Nurses, therapists, and surgeons work better when the patient is relaxed and confident. New England Baptist Hospital has a system that results in less stressed patients, which in turn causes less stress in staff, which causes less stress in patients, and so on.

What about holding on to those employees? Steve remembers: "The nurse, the physical therapist and the occupational therapist were all longtime employees. The nurse had been at New England Baptist since she graduated. I asked her, 'Have you ever thought about leaving?'

She said, "I would never want to leave here. I'm treated as a professional here. I'm not treated as a bedpan scrubber. The doctors respect us, the machines are where they should be, and when they break, they get fixed. We follow good protocols here, and there are never any surprises . . . except the medical ones, and that's what we're here for."

New England Baptist Hospital built a practice of finding and retaining the best employees—the keepers—by creating a virtuous cycle: build a great workplace with a unique culture, then use that workplace to attract the right people, then use those people to strengthen the culture, and use the culture to hold on to the people. Each part of this practice, from finding the best employees to treating them right to helping them create a culture that attracts more great employees, is deeply connected in a practice we call the Engagement Cycle.

Finding Keepers is Monster's guidebook to the Engagement Cycle.

Whatever your role as an employer—a hiring manager, an executive leader, a human resources generalist, an entrepreneur, or a full-time recruiter—you contribute vitally to this virtuous cycle of attracting, acquiring, and advancing the most skilled workers.

The central concept of *Finding Keepers* is this: good hiring is like good marketing. Not advertising, not selling, not sorting résumés . . . but marketing. That means understanding—reaching and serving the people you need in order to succeed. The difference is that marketers are trying to reach customers, and you are trying to reach, hire, and hold the most talented potential employees. To the hiring manager, the recruiter, the executive or human resources leader, "customers" are the rare, talented people who you want to join your company. To get them, you have to shift from focusing exclusively on your needs, and instead understand the needs, mindset, and behaviors of the most talented and productive employees.

Our job is to help you apply the principles and practices of the world's best recruiters to your organization. If there's one thing we at Monster have learned from talking to hundreds of thousands of managers like you, it's that the best hiring is built around the unique attributes of the organization. This makes your job much bigger than you might have thought, because it's really about transforming all your hiring practices to meet the bracing new set of business challenges that are roaring down the tracks right now. We'll detail those challenges in Chapter 1.

The Engagement Cycle is a powerful tool for small firms as well as big enterprises. As you'll see, small companies and not-for-profit organizations have advantages when it comes to this practice. They can often change more rapidly, respond more intimately to candidates, and develop an understanding of local talent recruiting that's hard for multinational corporations to do. At large organizations, the Engagement Cycle encourages even "B-level" employees to remain vital, flexible, and attached to the company. With more resources, a larger firm can deploy more of the practices we'll describe into the marketplace.

These techniques can be applied in your workplace, today. You don't have to work in a hot industry or a dominant company to get better at hiring and holding the best candidates. Certainly, we see expert practitioners around the world in every imaginable business.

In the course of writing a book for business users, questions of scope nag at every chapter. Should we stick to high-level ideas or try to prescribe a single recruiting system? Without underlying principles, a system has no guidance; without adaptation to realities on the ground, the principles don't gain traction.

We know the reality of recruiting: you have limited time and you have limited budgets. You might be the Cassandra of your company, warning that a talent shortage is about to harm the organization—but not empowered to change practices. If you are a hiring manager or an entrepreneur, you probably don't want to hear one more set of experts tell you to redesign the way you work, day to day . . . but you're going to have to do so to stay competitive.

Ultimately, a single prescription would be doomed to isolation, because excellent recruiting always reflects the culture, mission, stresses, and advantages of each business. We want you to apply the ideas in Finding Keepers to your hiring needs today. There are scores of practical actions and tips in this book that businesses of all sizes and any industry can use anywhere in the world. Where we have given models and tools to apply, they are meant as starting points for you to create a system that uniquely fits your situation.

Finding Keepers is a field guide to talent—attracting it, acquiring it, and advancing it within your organization. This book shows how to manage the relationship between talent and employer to gain a critical advantage over your competition. You'll learn the new power equation between candidate and employer, and meet innovators who are creating new ways to hire and hold the best. You'll meet leaders from Fortune 500 companies, small business owners, and dozens more from industries large and small. From hospital directors to diner owners, they're all experts in the art of finding, and holding, the best employees.

We Wrote This for You

More than 40 million job seekers trust Monster with their résumés, and we who work at Monster are grateful for their confidence. Less well-known to the general public than the site's popularity with job seekers is the fact that the core of Monster's business is the employer—the hundreds of thousands of managers like you who use Monster to attract and locate the right people to their organizations. They pay to advertise job openings on Monster. They search the site's résumé database, using Monster software and online tools to locate those "needle-in-a-haystack" candidates.

Building customer-focused practices has been coauthor Steve Pogorzelski's professional crusade. For almost two decades he's engaged deeply with people who do the hiring—people like human resources professionals, hiring managers, franchise owners, CEOs, and entrepreneurs. People like you. Steve is one of the key executives who has built a billion-dollar business solving your hiring challenges faster, cheaper, and better than your competitors. In the last few years, Steve has overseen the expansion of Monster's overseas businesses in more than two dozen countries. Each country has its unique employment laws, work customs, and economy; each faces the problem of a looming shortage of talented workers (even in the most populous countries).

To really serve its customers, Monster has to be more than job ads and résumés. It has to become an employer's partner in the never-ending tasks of improving hiring management and methods. Employers want to get better at hiring and retaining candidates. As you'll see, they have to get better in order to compete.

Note: For simplicity, we've used the terms *recruiter* and *employer* throughout the book to mean anyone involved in the practice of hiring.

To answer this need, coauthor Jesse Harriott created Global Monster Insights, a division focused on publishing actionable intelligence to help with strategic human resources planning. Jesse and his international team of experts conduct original research on the labor market and economic trends, as well as extensive research relevant to recruiting needs. The Monster Employment Index is published monthly in national, international, and local editions, and Monster Intelligence publishes free in-depth research and webinars throughout the year. You will find data, guidance, and insight from Jesse's special reports on subjects like diversity hiring, retention, employee engagement, and employment trends cited throughout *Finding Keepers*.

Since arriving at Monster in 1999, coauthor Doug Hardy's charter has been to offer actionable "how-to" information to help employers and job seekers make a better match. As Monster's first editor-in-chief, he presided over the publication of Web-based articles on every aspect of hiring. This book is his fifth collaboration for Monster.

Customer focus—professional research—making a better match. That's why we wrote this book. It's one more fulfillment of our promise to you to be more than an online medium but also an educational and consulting resource to make you better at hiring.

Thus, *Finding Keepers* is a guidebook, not a textbook. We hope that we got the balance right. Fortunately, because we work on the Web, we can and will add material that wouldn't fit into a book this size. You'll find a library of supplementary reports, webinars, and data at our Web site, http://intelligence.monster.com.

Chapter 1

The Quest for Quality

Business is in a worldwide competition to acquire a diminishing resource, an asset more valuable than oil and more critical than capital. The resource can be bought but not owned. It is found in every country but is difficult to extract. Leaders know that without this resource they are doomed to mediocrity, yet most of them use outdated methods of acquiring it.

The resource is skilled workers. In the United States alone, employers spend more than $250 billion a year locating, securing, and holding on to them. Internationally, companies large and small devote a similarly significant amount of money (as well as staff and executive time) to bringing in skilled workers and keeping them happy. Just one part of the process—help-wanted advertising—cost employers $20 billion globally in 2007.[1] Whether they're called employees, talent, human capital, or personnel, these are the people with the skills, work habits, knowledge, experience, and personal qualities that drive your business to its goals. These employees are rare by definition—the ones you want on your team whether you are on a hiring binge or managing layoffs. They are your keepers.

Keepers create the best new products. Keepers make the most revenue and find the greatest efficiencies. They build great workplaces, delight customers, and attract others like themselves to join the organization. They adapt to changing business conditions. Keepers are the most valuable talent—and finding, managing, and holding that talent is the key to your future. The Economist magazine's term "Quest for Quality" neatly summarizes the mission of business hiring, because high-quality talent can improve business performance at any stage of the business cycle.

You can't just go down to the talent store and buy a bunch of high-performing employees. As you will see, the underlying dynamics of locating, hiring, and retaining all employees—especially the best ones—call for a continuous give and take between employer and employee. Talent as a term goes beyond your current workforce to include people at every stage of the employment cycle. It includes potential employees who work elsewhere, candidates (those who might work for you), current employees, and former employees (alumni, including retirees and those who have left for other organizations).

If talent mattered less in the modern economy, the quest to find it would be less urgent. Today, it's the only long-term path to greater profits. That will be true tomorrow as well, due to three huge forces moving in the world economy.

Three Forces Set the Stage

We operate in an incredibly fluid and dynamic market for skilled workers. Three waves of change are converging worldwide to create a talent tsunami in the workforce, shifting power from the employer to the talented individual. Those three waves are (1) demographic changes, (2) candidate empowerment, and (3) the increasing value of talented employees relative to other success factors. Let's look at each one in turn.

Demographics

Predictions of a coming talent shortage are usually based on demographic data. Briefly, these data predict that retiring baby boomers won't be fully replaced by the workers that follow, thus creating a skills shortage—the usual number cited is a gap of about three million workers in the coming decade in the U.S. alone. (Government data are chiefly cited as the source of this figure.[2]) Low birthrates across the European Union and most countries of the Pacific, as well as the aging of populations across the industrialized world, will exacerbate these demographic trends in many world labor markets both now and in the long term.

In 2001, McKinsey & Co. published *The War for Talent*, which describes in detail the first talent shortage. The hiring slowdown around the year 2002 saw a brief pause, but a longer-term, global shortage of skilled talent quickly reappeared.

Numerous business sectors teeter on the edge of crisis even now: acute shortages of people capable of doing specific jobs in health care (for example, nursing, radiology, pharmaceutical), financial services, and technical management fields are driving up salaries and slowing growth. Squeezed by low numbers of science and engineering graduates on one side and disruptive technologies on the other, even the brashest entrepreneur lies awake worrying whether employees can be found who are talented enough to drive his or her vision.

Underlying these changes is the fact that schools aren't preparing enough people to fill the high-demand jobs. The number of science and engineering degrees in the United States has actually been on the decline for two decades, while jobs in those fields remain among the fastest growing.[3]

As globalization and international hiring expand, new educational issues arise. Language deficiencies are one obvious barrier to crossing borders. Educational quality also varies widely among countries. A 2005 McKinsey & Co. survey determined that only 13 percent of college graduates in low-wage countries were suitably qualified to work for multinational companies. Only 7 percent of Indian degrees are in engineering. The Czech Republic's educational system produces high-quality middle managers . . . but not enough of them to satisfy international demand.[4]

The health-care talent crisis actually accelerated in the recession years 2000–2001, because we just weren't creating enough health-care professionals to meet demand.[5] (Not only do we not have enough nurses, we don't have enough nursing teachers.[6]) Before the terrorist attacks on the United States on September 11, 2001, few predicted the boom in hiring for security, police, and government jobs; now it shows little sign of stopping. Wages are rising in these professions because there aren't enough qualified people to satisfy demand.

Moreover, new regulations and laws pressure employers. To cite two examples: the Sarbanes-Oxley regulations concerning corporate reporting create a need for more financial talent, and state laws capping patient-nurse ratios create a need for more nurses.

Demographic pressures range beyond white-collar professions. Jobs dominated by the baby-boom generation, such as qualified auto mechanics, will experience shortages caused by that group's general retirement. The trucking industry suffers today from a shortage of 20,000 drivers. Utilities can't find enough line workers.[7] A 2003 study by the National Association of Manufacturers described the disruptive effect of a skills imbalance in the workforce: "More than 80 percent of the surveyed manufacturers reported a 'moderate to serious' shortage of qualified job applicants."

Quick fixes won't solve the problem. Outsourcing changes some industries but actually only accounts for a small number of jobs compared to the overall labor force, as it has brought its own headaches. American and European women already lead the world in workforce participation rates, so entry of more women into the workforce won't be sufficient, even if it were an option for all families. Accelerated training for managers isn't a substitute for experience; you can't create a legion of managers with 10 years' experience overnight. There's a limited supply of experienced, intelligent, talented employees.

Can't business just import the talent from countries overseas? Not in sufficient numbers. In many countries, especially the United States and the European Union, immigrant workers are a political football both in terms of taking jobs from citizens and perceived national security concerns.[8] The United States has worked this territory for decades already, and according to the Society for

Human Resource Management, the United States already absorbs more than 50 percent of international labor flow, that is, people moving to another country to work.

Furthermore, competition for top talent is international. Skilled employees from Singapore to Spain don't just look to the United States, the European Union, and other countries for jobs, because skills shortages are cropping up in every developed country. A winter 2006 Manpower Inc. survey discovered that 40 percent of employers worldwide are having difficulty filling positions due to the lack of suitable talent available in their markets. India's university system is straining to supply domestic demand for graduates.[9] In 2005, a McKinsey & Co. paper on Chinese talent markets declared: "Our research points to a looming shortage. . . . A lack of locally-experienced talent managers and a growing trend toward wage inflation are hampering the efforts of companies to hire suitable staff in China."[10]

India and China have established themselves as players in the skilled talent market, creating an entirely new need to recruit globally. Europe is moving steadily toward American-style talent management, and despite higher overall unemployment rates than in the United States, Europe is currently experiencing shortages in certain areas.

Kent Kirch, head of global recruiting at Deloitte, says the demographic facts are especially foreboding in the developed economies: "The people we'll want to hire in 10 years have all been born, we can count them, we know their education level . . . and there aren't going to be enough. Japan and the major European economies are going to see a net reduction in the workforce over the next 20 years." Businesses in the developed countries are waking up to the reality that their own workers are being recruited by companies overseas, not just the other way around.

Candidate Empowerment

The second wave of change is the growing power of the candidate in the employment equation. The Internet makes it easy for any candidate, whether unemployed or working, to locate new opportunities quickly, research the company and salary, and quietly apply online. It has become much easier for employers to locate great candidates in online résumé databases, and tempt them away from their current organizations. In a free-agent marketplace, the stigma of "job-hopping" is all but gone. Talent can easily look to other regions or countries for opportunity.

Data tell the story. The average length of time someone spends in a job has shortened from 27 years in 1955 to barely four years today. A college graduate in 2006 can expect to hold 8 to 12 jobs over 40 years. Monster's recent employer surveys show that 50 percent of online job advertising is due to employee turnover, an indicator that talented people are on the move.

Business is threatened, moreover, by its point of view toward employees. Executives talk about "human capital assets" and then treat employees like assets—financial instruments that can be written off, disposed of, traded away, or deemed obsolete and simply dumped onto the market for whatever gain can be made.[11]

When people have a choice of jobs, they behave like consumers shopping among many products. If you want to attract the best, you have to compete for them. You have to offer them value. You have to understand why they might want to "buy" your company (that is, join your workforce). And then you have to get them to stay with you the same way that marketers gain loyalty—by offering them what they value, not once, but time after time.

> When people have a choice of jobs, they behave like consumers shopping among many products.

This new point of view is analogous to consumer marketing: you *attract* top talent with outreach, a strong brand message about your organization, and attractive work; you *acquire* talent by engaging it in a rewarding working relationship; and you *keep* talent by continuing to offer value over time, advancing the employee's career and life goals.

The new, empowered candidates distrust corporate culture. They remember how they and their parents were treated in the last couple of recessions—as "assets." Indeed, job seekers have long memories.

Increasing Relative Value of Talent

The third great wave affecting labor markets is the increasing value of talent to the bottom line, and the diminishing power of other assets to make a difference.

One by one the former advantages fall: capital flows much more freely than in the past; new products are quickly copied; workplaces become decentralized (so location matters less); former monopolies fail to compete. These structural changes don't mean the end of unemployment, but they do mean that talent is the remaining advantage.

Talent creates the lion's share of value in the developed world's companies, and those who calculate the intangible assets of organizations (know-how, patents, brand names, ideas, and processes) put the products of brainpower at 80 percent of a company's value.[12]

Globalization plays a part: As businesses in advanced economies cede manufacturing and low-end services to emerging economies, their survival depends on the products of high-end talent. Information-rich products and services, business innovation, sophisticated new technologies, better management, and more creative solutions drive first-world economies.

Recession only delays the reckoning; the structural shortages of talent will last much longer than any potential pause in hiring. Talented candidates ultimately have more choice of employers anywhere in the business cycle. The ability to attract and retain talent is an asset through boom and bust.

In a recession, employers have more bargaining power and a greater choice of candidates. During economic growth stages, bargaining power shifts toward the (talented) candidate. In any part of the cycle, those with in-demand skills command higher wages and other concessions. During the 2000–2002 recession period, employment and wages for nurses rose because of the chronic shortage.[13]

MY POV

"Some people in HR (human resources) or recruiting won't adjust their thinking until there's a crisis. But any of the data that you look at suggest that it's getting more and more difficult. The average length of time to fill a job is getting longer. And the average tenure of a person being in a job is shorter. Strong, strategic human resources leaders, managers, or professional recruiters really should understand that that's going to have an impact on their organizations and should start to think about the things they can be doing now to get ahead of it."

—*Linda Stewart, President and CEO, EPOCH LLC*

If no shortage of workers existed, this permanent change would increase the value of talent because talent is the last remaining factor that consistently delivers profits. Companies talk about innovation—it's talent that innovates. A retailer like Wal-Mart revolutionizes supply chain management and then discovers that midlevel store managers are the lynchpins that determine whether all that efficiently delivered merchandise gets bought. What determines whether your Web site will help deliver profits? The people who design, build, and grow your Web site.

The bottom line of finding keepers is the bottom line of your organization's existence: delivering profits (to a business) and/or fulfilling the mission (to a not-for-profit organization).

What to Do

How can an executive, recruiter, or manager find, hire, and retain top performers given these dynamics? How to compete in this marketplace? The quick response: pay more and spend more money looking for candidates. That solution might work for a while, and we're seeing it in wage pressure today, but a compensation arms race is not a long-term solution. You have to understand the skilled candidate's mindset and desires, and adjust.

The situation calls for a fully conceived, long-term practice of attraction using marketing disciplines and based on the understanding that talented workers view the employment market the way consumers consider a purchase. The new practice of recruiting attracts candidates by speaking their language, by communicating over the long term with many potential employees, and by studying their values, beliefs, and work motivations. The new practice of recruiting is mindful of the intangible as well as tangible benefits of employment and creates a vibrant, appealing "employer brand" to attract and acquire the right employees.

The rest of this book describes these new practices, how they work, and why they're critical for finding keepers:

1. **The candidate and the employer.** Understand the talent-as-consumer mindset, and prepare a more powerful, strategic set of business processes around the Engagement Cycle of Attract, Acquire, and Advance (Chapters 1–4).

2. **Attract.** Create compelling methods that locate and attract talent, not just to individual jobs but also to a great overall "employer brand" (Chapters 5–7).

3. **Acquire.** Bring a new understanding of the consumer mindset to all the processes that fall between first contact and hiring; study the global talent market; learn "next practices" in recruiting (Chapters 8, 10, and 11).

4. **Advance.** Boost your retention with a multidimensional, individualized program to keep the best employees engaged and productive and on your team (Chapter 9).

The quest for quality will determine whether your enterprise succeeds, survives, or fails in the coming decade. Those who integrate these principles to their particular business, culture, and mission will possess an abundance of the only remaining resource that matters—the human talent that is your company's future.

Review

- Three waves of change forces—demographic changes, candidate empowerment, and greater relative value of talent—are converging in a talent tsunami that threatens businesses for years to come.
- Short-term solutions won't ensure survival, much less prosperity.
- The winning response is to create a new practice of attracting, acquiring, and advancing talent that responds to skilled workers in the same way marketers respond to consumers.

Chapter 2

The New Candidate

Whatif the predictions are wrong? What if, despite the evidence, no shortage of skilled workers emerges?

Even if there were enough skilled workers to satisfy overall demand, managers would continue to compete for the *best* talent. Candidates and employees have to experience your organization as a fantastic place to work.

Build the team, hold onto it, and you'll win (even against the bigger competition). This sounds simple enough. If building a team were just a matter of picking players out of a lineup, it would be—but you don't have that choice. The candidate you want to hire isn't just standing in a lineup waiting to be picked.

The last two decades witnessed the end of the great postwar understanding between business and employees. Today's in-demand candidate is skeptical toward a company's promises of rewarding long-term work. Today's employee might enjoy or even love the company where she works, but she keeps a résumé online, an ear to the corporate rumor mill, and an eye on the door.

You're not in charge anymore.

The Candidate Is a Customer

In 1965, Ralph Nader's *Unsafe at Any Speed* sparked the modern consumer movement. American car buyers were outraged to learn that Detroit's manufacturers deliberately marketed defective and unsafe cars. Since then, every business has had to respond to the legacy of consumer skepticism (or even cynicism). Tobacco, food, household products, financial services, airlines, media, technology, mining, health care, funeral services, pharmaceuticals . . . every industry has endured its stories of deception and cover-up. Consumers stopped buying and demanded better treatment. Those companies that embraced accountability, honesty, and forthrightness did well. Those that actually listened to consumers prospered.

Beginning in the 1980s, employees experienced similar shocks to their belief in the great postwar bargain between business and employees ("work hard, be honest, and we'll take care of you"). Layoffs, reengineering, and the death of mutual loyalty created a different employee point of view. "Lifetime employment" was replaced by a lifetime employment *search* because people learned the hard way that all job positions are temporary. Even the government joined in: The military's "force reduction" in the early 1990s effectively brought layoffs to the army, and even when civilian government hiring expanded, rapid change meant less job security.

We've studied this consumer mindset in talented candidates from a number of perspectives, and it is manifest in an intriguing set of demands. Now that she has more choices, what (other than the right job) does she want from you?

The things a consumer wants from companies trying to market to her are respect for her time, candor, professional attention during the hiring process, prepared interviewers, truthful job advertisements, an efficient system, feedback all along the way (especially online), multiple ways to reach her, a clear message about what you want, tangible and intangible benefits at work, a fair deal, respect for her effort and her intelligence and talent, and much more. All of them flow from this new mindset that we call "poised."

Not Active, Not Passive, but Poised

Recruiters and hiring managers have long labeled potential employees by behavior—either they are "active" (that is, looking for a job) or "passive" (that is, employed and not looking). This bipolar model leads to pigeonholing candidates with a broad and inaccurate set of assumptions. For example, active candidates are supposedly less desirable than passive candidates because they're out of work or troubled at their jobs. This leads to ignoring highly qualified actives and focusing energy on recruiting passives, who are harder to interest, and who, in fact, are not necessarily more qualified than active candidates.

Managers, both in and out of recruiting, have bought into an 80/20 guesstimate; assuming 80 percent of the workforce is made up of those "passive" employees. In fact, the surprising truth is not an 80/20 division but a profile consisting of three distinct states of mind.

In 2006, Monster studied workers to assess these attitudes and help create a composite picture of employee loyalty. We discovered that the key factor is not whether someone is looking for a new job, but her level of attachment (or loyalty) to her current situation. Our understanding of workers' openness to switching jobs reveals a much larger group of potential candidates than the few who are actively looking for work. The largest segment of potential candidates—about 70 percent of them—consists of workers who are employed but much less attached to their current employer than workers historically have been. We found this segment across demographic categories, and it's especially true of the Generation X and Generation Y segments, the very ones who will be hired in greatest numbers in the coming decade.

The research finds these qualities among the three groups:[1]

1. ***Settled Loyalists (30 percent).*** These workers claim allegiance to their current job and employer. They are settled for a variety of personal and professional reasons. They are difficult to recruit, and they have high personal barriers to leaving their current position.

2. ***Poised Loyalists (11 percent).*** These are loyalists who claim allegiance to their current job and company but have a lower personal barrier to switching. A familiar example is the person who loves her work but has nowhere to go in a company or who dislikes the boss. This segment of the employed represents a vulnerability to their employers and an opportunity for recruiters.

3. ***Poised Opportunists (59 percent).*** These workers are clearly open to the next opportunity to change. They are open to approaches; they post their résumés online, reply to recruiting calls, or both. Many employed opportunists are actively looking for another job.

Today's poised workers—70 percent of the workforce—think of a job as a contract: they give their irreplaceable time, talent, and energy in return for tangible and intangible benefits: money, prestige, lifestyle benefits, and so forth. The arrangement lasts as long as both sides are satisfied. These workers tend to be less trusting of current employers, and they believe that better pay and benefits await them at other companies. As candidates, however, they have also learned to be skeptical of potential employers' claims. They have learned to question whether a job description reflects the reality of working day to day.

They will not tolerate bad bosses. They will make strong connections with good ones (in fact, this is a main line of defense against poised workers leaving, as you'll see in Chapter 9).

Poised workers are not disgruntled or mediocre—in fact, they are generally optimistic and see switching employers as a path to advancement. They don't seek job security from their current employer. They view security as a product of their own attractiveness to employers. Don't call them job-hoppers; most poised workers value stability and fewer transitions. They pay attention to the marketplace—building great résumés and posting them online, acquiring a broad range of skills and experiences, and networking. Their job changes tend to be moving up . . . on their terms, whether that's pay, job satisfaction, or fulfilling a lifelong dream. They're willing to change; research shows that among employed job seekers, 61 percent have had more than one full-time job in the past five years and 10 percent have had four or more jobs during this time.[2]

The 11 percent who characterize themselves as poised loyalists are positive about their jobs and bosses, but just because they feel loyal doesn't mean that they'll stay. For example, if a great boss leaves, the poised loyalists reporting to that boss might quickly lose their attachment to the company. Think of them as loyal to their individual situation, not to their employer in general.

Settled loyalists know the dynamics of the job market, and express their consumer mentality much as satisfied customers stay with trusted brands. They value their current compensation, work satisfaction, or personal situation, and those are high barriers to change. For loyalists, the risks of switching outweigh the benefits. It is possible to attract settled loyalists, but hiring them requires more incentives and persuasion than hiring similarly qualified poised workers.

Drop the model of active and passive and the old cutoff that says "if she's looking, something's wrong." It's misleading. Instead, seek poised workers where they are to be found, and determine each candidate's degree of attachment to his or her current situation.

The question someone on the hunt for talent should ask is not "who is looking (or not looking) today?" but "where can I find the best fit for this job and company today and tomorrow?" This question is always asked at the high levels of executive search, where few candidates are unemployed or looking, but many are open to change. Poised workers are in demand and have choices. The best outcome is to find a talented, poised candidate, bring her on, and over time convert her to a loyalist or even a de facto loyalist, that is, someone with a poised mindset but a situation so personally satisfying that other jobs suffer by comparison—what you might call "psychological golden handcuffs."

Imagine filling your critical positions with people like that.

Poised Employees = Your Employees

Why build a quest for quality employees around the poised candidate? Because these are *your* employees! No company is immune to the realities of the new employee/candidate mindset. The bad news is you cannot take loyalty for granted. The good news is that your employees themselves can help you understand the needs and desires of the poised workforce.

Still think you're different? In the early days at Monster, we got a lot of pushback from companies that said, "I know you have a lot of résumés in your database, but they're not the kind of people I want to hire." We would say, "Okay, let's just look here in the database for people who are currently working at your company. . ." We would do this with a big company, and up would come a thousand résumés. They were totally shocked. Then we'd say: "You can't go to these employees and accuse them of disloyalty. The world has changed. Unless you can guarantee them a job for life—and you can't—then career management is up to them." Then the light would go on in the recruiters' eyes because they could see that the people they wanted to reach could be a lot like the people they already had. And their best people were poised for the same reasons they were high performers: they took initiative, knew their worth, and took responsibility for their own careers.

More than two-thirds of your employees are in a "poised" mindset, and even if they're not looking for a new job, they're fair game for your competitors.

Monster's research also uncovered surprising disconnects between what candidates want and what employers think candidates want. Take a moment to study Table 2-1.[3]

Table 2-1

Perspectives on What Job Seekers Want in a Position*

	Job Seeker	Hiring Manager	Staffing Director
Opportunities to learn and grow	78%	68%	69%
Interesting work	77%	63%	63%
A good manager/boss	75%	69%	57%†
An organization you can be proud to work for	74%	58%	55%
Opportunity to advance	73%	69%	77%
Promise of stability/job security	70%	62%	65%
A creative or fun workplace culture	67%	50%	43%
A compatible work group/team	67%	50%	37%
Balance between work and personal life	65%	65%	65%
Opportunity for accomplishment	64%	53%	41%

*Beyond salary and benefits
†Underrated

For example, as Table 2-1 reveals, while only 50 percent of hiring managers believe a creative or fun workplace culture is important to candidates, 67 percent of candidates rate it as important. Only 41 percent of staffing directors believe an opportunity for accomplishment is important, whereas 64 percent of candidates want that in a position (and 69 percent of staffing directors believe an opportunity to learn and grow is important . . . but don't connect that to accomplishment). No wonder so much hiring leads to quick attrition—hiring managers are bringing in employees without knowing what they really want. Result: employee frustration and high turnover.

> *More than two-thirds of your employees are in a "poised" mindset, and even if they're not looking for a new job, they're fair game for your competitors.*

We find another disconnect in assessing flight risk. When managers rate how many employees are at risk for leaving the company, they typically come up with a figure of 3 percent or 5 percent, but the actual figure of people leaving voluntarily is three, four, or five times

MY POV

"To a candidate, the decision to work for you is going to be one of the most important decisions she makes in the coming years. It's very much like a considered purchase, like buying a house. A smart candidate wants to make a decision with an educated and informed mind. She's only going to come to work for you if she trusts you. So the question is, how is a hiring manager to build that level of trust? I don't think managers pay enough attention to building trust with talented candidates, but it's a critically important factor in a successful hire."

—Jim Lanzalotto, VP of Strategy and Marketing, Yoh

that. It's not because managers aren't able to count—it's because the dominant view of "passive" candidates clouds their assumptions. They assume that if employees are doing their job and collecting their pay, they are happy. The facts say otherwise.

Assume that 70 percent of your workforce is poised; you have to earn their loyalty every day. Then assume that 70 percent of your competitors' workforces are also poised, and think of the opportunity to earn their interest, and perhaps their loyalty as well.

Generational Perspectives

Another perspective on the candidate–employee pool focuses on three large demographic groups in the workforce today. Segmenting candidates by age and experience offers insight to their expectations.

Our research shows that younger, less-experienced employees approach the job market with a fresh perspective and high levels of optimism as they set out to build their careers. Older, more seasoned employees tend to be more established in their careers and satisfied with their day-to-day work, but some might be less trusting of management and more cynical about the job market overall.

Baby Boomers (Born 1946–1964): Productive, Expert, Changing

David Corbett, founder of career transition firm New Directions, would like to abolish the word retirement. It's an inadequate description, he says, for what the generation born from 1946 to 1964 intends to do in the coming years.

Dave's executive clientele includes accomplished boomers looking for a change and recent retirees who find their way to his harborside offices because going from 70 hours of work every week to a lifetime on the golf course doesn't make sense. Instead of leaving work entirely, Dave says, they aspire to a "portfolio life" of activities including work, family, recreation, education, and service.

As boomers continue their careers after age 50, "you have to play to their changing priorities," says Dave. "They check their lives every couple of years like a financial portfolio, rebalancing the pieces. You have to understand their changing motivations, particularly when they become empty nesters."

Boomers are the country's largest repository of talent and experience, and that's why their exit from the workforce will cause so much pain for companies. Corbett's clients, however, are saying that they don't so much want to exit the workforce as participate in a different way. Recruiters who adjust can capture that talent. The following is a portrait of the oldest generation of active workers.

The oldest baby boomers just hit 60, the youngest are in their 40s, and boomers still make up the largest age sector of the workforce—42 percent, or about 48 million employees. Due to their longer experience on the job, these employees tend to be highly productive, and many have developed great expertise and judgment through the years.

Like their elders, many boomers have been whipsawed by the changes in workplace life. They have straddled the information revolution, having been educated in a pre-PC world and now fully ensconced in work technology. They have had to change their understanding of job security, retirement planning, and personal mobility. They have become adaptable.

Research by Monster shows that boomers are aware of the competition of the generations that have followed them. Boomers are more expensive to hire and retain than younger candidates, and they believe this puts them at a competitive disadvantage. A full 70 percent in our survey agree with the statement "if two people with the same qualifications are competing for a job, usually the younger person gets hired."

A hiring manager can address this issue by predicting and comparing the productivity of a more-experienced worker versus a beginner in the same job. The productivity of an older candidate (who has a quantifiable track record) might well be more predictable than a younger one. The hiring manager who wants to exploit a boomer's experience needs to think about value (what you get for your money) as well as price.

When they do look for new positions, boomers are more focused on tangible benefits like health insurance and retirement plans.[4] They are less focused on career growth. Flexibility, for example, in the form of work-at-home arrangements, is an important factor to older workers when they are deciding between offers, as they cope with the sandwich-generation demands of caring for children and aging parents.

More-experienced workers also tend to be more satisfied with their current jobs, and in our surveys 78 percent said they anticipate being in their current job in a year. Compared to younger workers, more-experienced employees feel positive about their company's culture; they feel better about their managers, more valued, and more respected than their younger peers. They also tend to be less tolerant of poor management, more risk-averse, and doubtful of job security.

One interesting factor that varies with age is whether an employee admires her manager. One would expect this to be more important to younger employees who seek out role models. However, as with benefits, this resonates more strongly with older employees.[5] It suggests that older workers, given their experience, set a higher standard for management behavior.

Generation X (Born 1965–1977): Transition Generation

Generation X, which swept into the job market just after the old model of job security crumbled, values self-reliance. Somewhat tempered by the blind enthusiasms of the late 1990s (the "this time it's different!" era), Generation Xers remain a powerhouse of innovation, knowledge, and skill. This comes as no surprise, as the formative working years of Generation Xers have coincided with the business revolutions of the 1980s, 1990s, and 2000s [namely: In Search of Excellence, reengineering, Six Sigma, customer relation management (CRM), and long booms in both productivity and economic growth]. This generation has discovered the joy of creativity on the job, and learned how to combine discipline with creativity.

Although Generation Xers doubt that a long-term relationship is possible with any one employer, they are adept at gaining a range of experiences, and they view work as a place to learn and grow. They are more entrepreneurial than boomers, but that doesn't necessarily draw them to start-ups only. As they invest in mortgages, families, and other long-term commitments, they also settle into careers, building a personal roster of skills and expertise, which they intend to leverage in the marketplace. Just turning 40 now, the early curve of Generation Xers is in a talent market sweet spot, with a record of accomplishment that increases their value and the flexibility to move to a better job. Work-life balance issues tend to reflect the responsibilities of early family life (for example, still willing to work long hours and be held to high standards, but interested in telecommuting).

As baby boomers are interested in the meaning of their work, Generation Xers strive for *efficacy*—accomplishments that confirm the work and learning they have achieved. They are intolerant of bureaucracy and reject projects that will never see the light of day.

Generation Xers are also brand-conscious and brand-savvy. With so many products competing for their attention, Generation Xers use brands to decide where they'll give their attention. Employers must develop a powerful and authentic employer brand to get their attention (see Chapter 5).

Generation Y (Born 1978 and After): Millennial Mobility

Generation Y, or the Millennials, entered the workforce in the last 10 years. They are steeped in technology and living online. Generation Y is the smallest, but fastest-growing, sector of the workforce, and they are your future talent. Even more brand-conscious (and marketing-drenched) than the preceding generations, Millennials must be approached with a deliberate and authentic message about your company.

This cohort has the lowest barrier to switching jobs. They are less settled in one location, and they see switching jobs as a fast path to advancement. Generation Yers also migrate from place to place online, as the changing popularity of Friendster, MySpace, Facebook, and other social networking sites attests. In fact, the computer screen isn't a barrier. Yesterday they were found on personal Web sites; tomorrow they might find their job on a cell phone text message or a multimedia experience on a handheld computer.

Bruce Tulgan of Rainmaker Thinking studies the Millennials, and he emphasizes the importance of high expectations in the youngest cohort of workers. They expect a lot of achievement from themselves and demand more flexible work arrangements with employers. In Bruce's words, "Generation Y will be the most high-maintenance workforce in the history of the world and they'll also be the most high-performing workforce."

Don't confuse high expectations with a disrespectful sense of entitlement (the source of a million "I don't know what's wrong with kids today" ruminations by older managers). Some individuals will always feel entitled to more. Instead, recall that Generation Y is the first to grow up in the shadow of the new job insecurity. These people saw parents and older siblings work long hours and then get laid off anyway. They saw the dot-com boom and bust.

Lori Erickson, Monster's senior vice president of global human resources, asserts that Generation Y workers are keenly observant of the changing scene. She says: "A Gen Y candidate is not just fixated on pay, but deeply desires flexibility around work-life balance issues. Job content is critical—the ideal job has to be interesting and challenging. Gen Y employees also think about advancement—more skills, faster promotion. Compared to the older generations, immediate money is less seductive. They're not as caught up in the promises of enormous IPO [initial public offering]-based fortunes like so many of their parents and older siblings. They saw how rarely that really happens."

Although they are on the opposite side of the generational timeline from the baby boomers, they also place high value on the nonmaterial rewards of work—they want meaning in their work, and a sense that their contribution matters. Like Generation X workers, they appreciate flexible work schedules, but whereas a Generation Xer wants time for family and outside responsibilities, Generation Y members want time for personal growth and self-expression.

More than their predecessors, the Millennials live online. Because they take information technology for granted, they assume that formerly hard-to-get information (such as salary data) is a few clicks away. Their technological savviness also leads to impatience with hard-to-use corporate recruiting sites.

Dan Taylor, a former recruiter for DialogueDirect fundraising, found young graduates almost entirely by reaching them online. DialogueDirect maintains a page on MySpace.com, where candidates, employees, and idle watchers post their own comments. The site can appear chaotic to outsiders, but DialogueDirect's presence is as much the message as its particular pitch. Many candidates express interest after visiting the site, but attracting candidates is only part of the overall experience.

"I try to think like a single 22- to 24-year-old male that just came home from a concert last night and doesn't have a job," says Dan. "My job is to get out in front of those kids, in exactly the right place to say 'here's something you didn't think of before: fundraising for charities out on the street.'"

They Don't Think What You Think They Think

Individuals are different from groups, and you'll always be able to find a 60-year-old online networking enthusiast or a 22-year-old Luddite. There's always the chance that a loyalist employee at your competitor will want to join you. Hiring is not a game of ferreting out exceptions, however; it's a game of identifying the exceptional.

Ultimately, hiring great talent requires you to customize your approach, and when you know the preferences of a group, you can craft a better message to individuals. This goes for understanding the poised versus loyal potential candidate, the three large age cohorts, and the candidate with qualifications that are scarce. The same can be said for diversity hiring (see Chapter 11), or hiring to fit a particular corporate culture. We doubt that employers on the whole have learned too much about employees, and good recruiting, like a good marketing campaign, begins with knowing who you want to reach, and why.

Our surveys frequently discover gaps between management's estimation of employee loyalty and the actual loyalty of the workforce.

Where's the disconnect here? It lies in the anecdotal evidence managers and human resources so frequently rely on. The exit interview is an example of a good idea often badly executed. In a typical exit interview, an employee will say she's leaving for more money. But when the headhunter called that person a month before, the employee said that her boss was a nut or that there weren't enough challenges in her current job. Lacking true quantification, management convinces itself that each individual has individual reasons to leave . . . but that doesn't tell the broader story.

True loyalists and even poised loyalists say their good relationship with their boss is a reason to stay, and opportunists typically say they are frustrated with their manager, cynical about executive management, or otherwise not buying into the company's story.

Another disconnect: 60 percent of workers we surveyed believe that companies other than their employer offer greater salary and benefits for the same work.[6] Yet most companies believe they offer competitive salary and benefits (indeed, most of them have to, in order to compete for talent). The threat arises when executive management believes that facts speak for themselves and forgets that hiring and holding talent is as much about telling a story as it is about facts. In the next chapter, you'll see how the insights of good marketers can inform the quest for quality.

In fairness to management, we'll add that the situation isn't improved by the lack of candidate knowledge, especially in the early years of a career. Go to high school and talk to a 17-year-old boy—he has no idea he can make $75,000 a year as an auto body mechanic. He might spend every weekend restoring his 1968 Camaro. He'll go to college and major in art history and never consider auto mechanics as a career. Instead, he'll look for a job in the arts, which are rare, then go to work in someone's customer service telephone center for $30,000 a year. And in six months he'll quit. In fact, if that kid dropped his preconceptions of what he should do, and instead pursued a career that reflected his true value and his true happiness, he would be more fulfilled, and an auto body shop would have higher profits. He'd also make a good living because America faces a critical shortage of auto body mechanics. (Remember that the next time you drive and while talking on your cell phone.)

Jim Yang, Monster account manager for China, points out that similar mismatches happen in other cultures. For example, "When a new five-star office building goes up in Shanghai, candidates want to work there and they'll disregard more appropriate job opportunities at less prestigious locations."

Respond to Reality

Sometimes it seems as if candidate–employees and managers live in different, universes. As you'll see in Chapter 3, however, the managers who understand their candidates' and employees' universe will find that an expanded view of recruiting neatly parallels the contemporary candidates' view of career management. The manager who learns to reach out to candidates, employees, and alumni in the right ways, and at the right times, can develop long-term relationships with the most talented workers.

The new candidate is on the move today but ultimately looking for a home. It's a question of reaching across that gap into their world, at the right times, in the right ways, and with the right understanding.

Review

- Today's candidate attitudes are similar to today's consumer attitudes.
- Target potential candidates by understanding the "poised" mindset, not transitory "active" or "passive" behaviors.
- Generational differences in mindset are a major criterion for determining your approach.
- Employers must test their assumptions, because the disconnect between what employees think and what management believes employees think is often large, especially with the poised worker.

Chapter 3

The Engagement Cycle

The quest for quality drives hiring. Great hiring results in higher profits and growth.[1] Great talent, always hard to find, is getting more elusive, but finding and keeping a talented workforce is a sustainable competitive advantage. It can be done. The situation calls for a change in how you hire—not just tweaking around the edges, but a permanent shift in thinking and tactics.

Most employers behave as if hiring is a one-week string of transactions: I post a job ad, you reply. We talk and if I like you, I hire you.

From the employee's point of view, that's just a snapshot in a much longer set of changing relationships. First he is a potential employee, then a candidate, then an employee at your company, and later an alumnus of your company. You must think from a marketer's perspective about this evolution, because it is the key to building a hiring practice that's relevant to the candidate.

Think Like a Marketer

Three forces drive the quest for quality: demographic changes, candidate empowerment, and the greater relative value of talent. These forces give poised workers more choice and therefore more power in the hiring relationship. If you are among the 70 percent of managers who is in a poised mindset, you understand this concept at a gut level. More choice in the job market is like more choice in the supermarket—many products chasing the same consumers.

So the task for the employer is to turn "consumer" candidates into "customers" who will "buy their product," that is, join their organization. This is a dramatic change in thinking for most people.

When we ask managers to raise their hands if they believe a skills shortage is coming, most raise their hands. When we then ask "how many of you think of yourselves as marketers? How many understand that candidates and employees are customers whose loyalty has to be earned?" less than 5 percent raise their hands.

"But you're in the attraction and retention business," we say. "How can you not think like a marketer? Do you think the talent you need is going to come to your doorstep just because you put a job posting up?"

Peter Drucker wrote, "True marketing starts . . . with the customer; his demographics, his realities, his needs, his values. It does not ask, 'What do we want to sell?' It asks, 'What does the customer want to buy?'"[2] Marketers spend a lot of time thinking about how to find the best potential customers, understand as much as possible about them, and give them what they want over the long term. They study and classify segments of customers, identifying the most valuable. They tailor their products and services to satisfy the needs of the best customers.

In just the same way, great hiring identifies high-value employees and tailors recruiting, hiring, management, and retention strategies toward these employees. With strong hiring, managers can build a strong base of motivated, talented, and flexible employees.

For example, the consumer brand Oakley emphasizes rugged outdoor recreation when marketing its products. Its high-value customers are turned on by Oakley's images of strenuous sports—rock climbing, mountain biking, and the like—and a strong attitude. Young women in Oakley videos say, "I'm not waiting for your approval . . . I live by my own rules." L.L. Bean, by contrast, seeks to attract a different customer, and its marketing emphasizes an easier, less rebellious, more settled attitude. Distinct customers, distinct messages.

Now look at the differences between two tough-minded hiring organizations with a similar recruiting challenge: the U.S. Marine Corps and the U.S. Army. On the surface, they give similar messages to attract recruits (who are in fact employees): we're looking for brave and dedicated men and women who want to serve their country. But their messages are carefully tailored to quite different mindsets. The Marines emphasize exclusivity, tradition, pride, and a life-long sense of belonging to the corps. The Army puts more emphasis on opportunity, career preparation, and rewards (educational benefits, for example). Again—distinct audiences, distinct messages.

Marketers communicate to customers through brands. They create brands with specific and unique attributes that will attract, satisfy, and delight customers. They describe brands in terms of benefits for the customer, and, in the same way, employers must learn to describe the employment relationship in terms of benefits for the employees. We'll show you Monster's method for doing this in Chapter 5.

The Engagement Cycle

As companies move from the hiring-as-transaction view to the marketing view, we see that employer and candidate follow a clear three-phase cycle in the course of their working relationship. These three phases describe the level and quality of engagement between employee and employer, which we call the Engagement Cycle:

1. **Attract.** The Attract phase is a long-term "dance" between you and the candidate. It includes every activity meant to position the organization as a potential employer in the mind of a candidate. You project a carefully crafted, authentic image as an employer; they become aware of your organization's specific attributes. Your employees spread your reputation as an employer; the candidate listens and assesses you as a potential work-place. It's a similar dance to the way consumers are drawn to brands in the marketplace.

2. **Acquire.** This phase involves all the interactions between you and candidates from the moment they reach out to you. You advertise a position and they apply. You treat their application a certain way, and they react. You find their résumé and approach them, and they judge you by your image and your behavior. Your interview process is a series of interactions with different parts of your organization. Both candidate and employer set expectations throughout this process that will be critical in making a good hire and later in holding onto the best talent. The Acquire stage also includes the honeymoon period right after an employee starts working, in which expectations will be tested against reality. In terms of consumer branding, this is the purchase of a product and its aftermath: Does the product perform as advertised? Is the customer so satisfied that he would recommend the product?

3. **Advance.** Keep critical talent moving, not necessarily up, but growing in experience, responsibility, money, or other tangible and intangible ways. Advancing talent in your organization is a key to retaining good people and vital to your company's ability to change as opportunity or necessity require. Retention is the "hold" part of hire and hold; in consumer branding terms, it's the equivalent of customers becoming loyal to a brand and identifying with the brand's attributes.

The Engagement Cycle is the long-term flow of activities that attract, acquire, and advance talent, and it is the interplay of the full cycle—both the employer's three activities and the candidate's responses—that creates a strong relationship. Figure 3-1 shows the concurrent activities from the employer and candidate points of view.

The first stage—Attract—consists of getting the word out and identifying the consumer-minded candidates' activities in a job search (including checking you out). The middle stage—Acquire—is transactional and relatively brief. In the third phase—Advance—both sides try to maximize the value of the relationship.

Figure 3-1

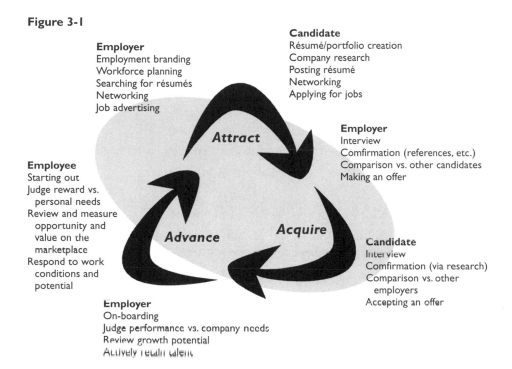

Employer
Employment branding
Workforce planning
Searching for résumés
Networking
Job advertising

Candidate
Résumé/portfolio creation
Company research
Posting résumé
Networking
Applying for jobs

Employer
Interview
Comfirmation (references, etc.)
Comparison vs. other candidates
Making an offer

Employee
Starting out
Judge reward vs.
   personal needs
Review and measure
   opportunity and
   value on the
   marketplace
Respond to work
   conditions and
   potential

Candidate
Interview
Comfirmation (via research)
Comparison vs. other
   employers
Accepting an offer

Employer
On-boarding
Judge performance vs. company needs
Review growth potential
Actively retain talent

This last phase might repeat over the time that an employee works at your company. A poised worker is always judging the employer against other potential employers. When talent is in demand, you have to re-earn its engagement constantly or risk losing it to someone else.

The Engagement Cycle requires more attention than transactions because it is multidimensional and depends on the ongoing interaction. For example, it's not enough for your outreach to be good; how you receive the candidate's response is also important.

The Attract phase can last for years. For the career-minded worker, employment is not a single event but a sequence of encounters: a candidate hears about
an employer, maybe years before applying for a job there (but from the moment
the candidate hears, he starts to form an impression). In the language of marketing, that's a touch point. Sometime later the candidate hears about the company from a friend who works there. That's another touch point. Perhaps he
then uses one of the company's products, or shops in its store; that's another
touch point. Then the candidate connects in a very specific way to an opportunity—a job advertisement, a network contact, a call from a recruiter who dug
up his résumé. More touch points. Then the candidate applies for the job and
goes through the process of getting the job. More touch points. Then he starts
working as an employee, and he's now in a daily relationship with the employer
until he leaves the company—retires, quits, is let go, or dies.

Jennifer Tracy of Limited Brands describes a couple of low-key touch points
that were carefully orchestrated to send the right message:

> We knew an individual at a company overseas, identified as hot talent in the
> visual space. We were able to get the person on the phone and say—hey, you
> know, let's just start a relationship. The recruiter had a coffee with the
> individual when they happened to be in the same city, and after we had that
> conversation, we realized this person was an A player. So we set up another
> informal meeting, this time with an executive, the head of our visual design
> practice, just to talk about what might happen three months, six months
> down the road. A personal conversation with an executive, with no
> pressure—that's the kind of thing that makes the difference to candidates.

Most companies focus all their hiring effort on the brief Acquire phase that
takes place around a job opening. Perhaps that's because there's obvious room
for improvement here in skills like interviewing, writing effective goals and job
descriptions, and the like. It's also a phase that has a clear decision point, and
one that lends itself easily to measurement (How many people did you interview? How long did it take?). Landing talent that's in demand, however, begins

with getting better talent interested in coming to work for you, and that begins long before you have an empty seat crying to be filled.

What is "Advance" doing in a book about hiring? That's the "Keepers" part of *Finding Keepers*. Retention is a burning issue in the minds of good employers, who work hard to keep their best employees. Employers know their competition is working hard to get them. Advance is the win-win of great hiring, as employers get increasing returns on their people investment and employees get more skills, more experience, and more money.

We haven't lost sight of the irony every good manager experiences—increasing the value of a keeper also makes him more valuable to the competition. But that's an acceptable risk. The potential downside of losing a good employee doesn't justify holding that person back. What are you going to say: "We kept turnover really low by making sure our people are less productive than the competition's people."?

> *The Engagement Cycle is a multidimensional, long-term approach to hiring and holding skilled employees.*

The military has lived a long time with this deal. Military service teaches skills readily applicable to business. Some service members make a career in the military, and many transfer their skills to the private sector. The positive attrition—loss of people because their value has increased—is the price of improved performance for the military.

Even though highly talented employees rarely lose the poised mindset, there are many things you can do to keep those people. This is the long-term job of Advance, which we'll cover in Chapter 9.

Recruiting, Marketing, and Management

Hiring is typically treated as business processes disconnected from the functioning of the rest of the company, as if supplying and supporting talent were an isolated process like supplying and supporting phone service.

Marketing is seen differently:

- Marketing is the bridge between the customer and the company.
- Marketing's message to the customer must reflect authentic value.
- Marketing is responsible for understanding the customer . . . not just once but over and over.
- Marketing guides the experience of the customer.
- Marketing creates a relationship with the customer that inspires loyalty.
- Marketing identifies people who might be customers a year from now.
- When customers leave, or reject the company's offering, marketing has to figure out why.

MY POV

"Talent acquisition is nothing more than a supply chain. For the recruiter, it's all about the suppliers, and then it's about the quality of product that you get in, and then it's about delivering to your customers (the managers in your organization) as quickly as possible. We brought in applicant tracking systems and we mapped and modeled all our processes. So we had a real predictive supply chain.

"Then we looked at our strategy going out a few years, and when you do that you can identify workforce gaps—not just projected turnover, but also growth. This is a whole lot better than the typical calls saying, 'Dan, I need 30 engineers, and I need them yesterday!'"

—Dan Hilbert, Valero Energy
and Orca Eyes, Inc.

Now, change just two words in the list above, and you've listed the practical tasks of the Engagement Cycle:

* *Management* is the bridge between the *candidate* and the company.
* *Management*'s message to the *candidate* must reflect authentic value.
* *Management* is responsible for understanding the *candidate*, not just once, but over and over.
* *Management* guides the experience of the *candidate*.
* *Management* creates a relationship with the *candidate* (as *employee*) that inspires loyalty.
* *Management* identifies people who might be *candidates* a year from now.
* When *candidates* leave, or reject the company's offering, *management* has to figure out why.

This is the "marketing" work of managing talent: understand the wants, needs, and promise of individuals and adjust your "product" (that is, a position at your company) according to both their needs and yours.

The Engagement Cycle means "recruiting" never stops. It means some of the sacred cows of an organization (like traditional work and compensation plans) might have to change. In some cases it means making small adjustments such as creating new positions outside the management structure for talented individuals. Other situations might call for more sweeping moves, such as taking an honest and systematic look at whether current hiring messages and methods are bringing in people who have the potential to remain engaged.

The promise of an Engagement Cycle practice is worth the effort to change both hiring and managing systems. In a worldwide shortage of talent, the cycle of attracting, acquiring, and advancing talent has the power of a great marketing campaign, building long and growing relationships with customers. You will get the right people into the right positions, and create the right conditions for them to flourish.

The Engagement Cycle doesn't happen overnight, but it can be achieved one piece at a time. The first step in this journey is deciding where you are. That's the subject of the next chapter.

Review

- For hiring managers to think like marketers, they have to understand and manage details of the candidate experience.
- The experience follows three phases, beginning much earlier and ending much later than the traditional, transactional hiring process.
- Management must take responsibility for the candidate experience along every phase of the Engagement Cycle, including the post-hiring phase.

Chapter 4

Where Are You Today?

When it comes to transforming recruiting from art to science, Dan Hilbert of Valero Energy (a large oil refining and marketing corporation) is one of the best practitioners around. As a former entrepreneur, this human-resources expert knows the value of rigorous, numbers-driven analysis.[1]

Hilbert asserts that creating an indisputable business case for good hiring is an elusive goal, but today's lack of a grand unified formula for human capital valuation is no excuse for inaction. Dan gave us an example of his thinking recently:

> Everyone's trying to figure out the true value of human capital. There's got to be a way to link the people to the business. I don't have a perfect answer,

but I can sure link high-impact, mission-critical positions directly to revenue, directly to strategic business objectives, directly to corporate and operations and drivers, and directly to core business risks or primary business risks.

What's a high-impact position? It's someone who directly impacts a disproportionately high level of revenue and strategic objectives, your core business operations, or primary business risks. These are the difference makers; these are your stars you put on the court to play against other companies every day.

I'll give you an example: oil refineries take an enormous amount of energy to run. So when energy costs go up, we get hit just like everyone else. We hired five energy-use experts, and told them, "You're each responsible for saving $20 million a year in energy costs for the next five years." Let's do some easy math: each one of these people is responsible for saving $100 million in energy costs. Valero stock currently has a 7-to-1 price-to-earnings ratio. When you multiply that $100 million by 7, you're saying they are each responsible for adding $700 million of shareholder value over the next five years . . . cumulatively $3.5 billion of shareholder value.

Hilbert knows that this kind of thinking isn't restricted to executive leadership. His analysis continues:

Refinery executives realize that one of the highest-impact positions in their business is the welder. Why? We've got these 300-foot towers that are filled with thousands of barrels of crude oil. The oil is burning at over 1,000 degrees, and if one of these bolts comes loose at the wrong time at the wrong place, you're going to have a really bad day. A great welder knows exactly when to say, "Hey, at the 22nd floor, in that corner, in this weather . . . I need to go check that weld."

I modeled the value of a welder based on how hard they are to recruit, compared to the risk of not having one. I realized in many ways we've got a bigger problem getting these skilled technicians than we do getting white-collar professionals. We've defined 14 positions that are critical for the success of our refineries in the coming years . . . and that demographic statistics tell us will face a shortage. Now, we are proactively targeting and attracting people with these skills, so that before we need them, we'll be connected with them. We're even open to bringing some of them in before they're needed, or even bringing in younger ones to more developmental positions so that when the refineries need them, they will be ready.

To reach this more elusive set of core talent, Dan built closer relationships with technical colleges and high schools, making sure that skilled welders knew about Valero even before they graduated. Yes, he recruits at the best business schools as well, but his knowledge of where the value of his company lies leads Dan to search in the right places for the right people.

Your situation is similar to Dan Hilbert's, whether you work in a multinational energy corporation or a 30-person retail shop. If you want to find great people and keep them, you have to approach the Engagement Cycle of Attract, Acquire, and Advance with an understanding of where you are today and where you have to be tomorrow. You have to make the case for change, decide where to put your resources, and then go after the employees who will make the greatest difference to your business.

The Engagement Cycle gains momentum over time as better recruiting attracts more talented candidates. Performance improves, which in turn makes the organization more attractive to the best. You see this virtuous cycle come to life in a hot company, such as Google which, with about 10,000 employees, receives 100,000 job applications a month.

Planning how to attract, acquire, and advance the *right* people begins with a bit of organizational self-discovery, so before you start writing persuasive statements about why your organization is the best place in the world to work, you have to determine the answers to some fundamental questions. You need to know who is most critical to your company's success, what they want, how they succeed, and why they stay or leave. You have to make people and processes accountable for results. To those who think they really understand their current workforce, and the effectiveness of their hiring, we ask:

- Are you satisfied with your current employees?
- Are you growing, maintaining, shrinking, or reorganizing your workforce?
- Are the leaders of your organization committed to building the best possible workforce, beyond the usual lip service?
- If you or they were funding a new business today, with your own money, would you hire the same people and put them in the same jobs?
- Where does your hiring system excel, and where does it break down? What role does technology play? From printing paychecks to searching for résumés to operating a full-blown "talent management system," you use some level of information technology in hiring.
- Who are your most valuable employees?
- What do your most valuable employees have in common?
- How do you decide if job A is more important than job B?
- Are your hiring budgets and behavior aligned accordingly? This is especially important in growing businesses, where we often notice a "cult of indispensability" forming around core departments.
- Do you really know the cost of your turnover, not just in the number of employees who have to be replaced every year, but the total cost?
- Are the right employees staying, and are the right ones leaving?
- Are key employees leaving because they're lured away for more money than you can afford or because poor management is killing interest, loyalty, and engagement?

All this comes down to the beliefs and actions of key people in your organization—executives, managers, recruiters, human resources professionals, and yes, employees. Is each aware of her role in the quest for quality? Is her contribution to a better workforce a priority? Are managers compensated for improving the quality of the employee base?

Specific and candid answers to these questions lead to better hiring practices. Whether you work with 22,000 employees or 22, the answers to these questions are unique to your organization's particular mix of resources, management techniques, strategy, culture, and values. Profits can flow from great customer service, operational excellence, product innovation, marketing, or other factors, but in every case, the quality of your people determines the size of your profit.

Execute a hiring strategy disconnected from your current reality and you are going to be frustrated. You've seen the mistakes: organizations that need great line managers but load up on strategists; companies that should improve their customer service but keep offering new products because they started with a group of product builders; mature companies needing a more sophisticated sales approach continuing to add only entry-level sales staff; and so on.

Executives, line managers, and human resources professionals need to know the capabilities of the workforce in vivid detail, for only then can they make needed adjustments.

There are actually two broad capabilities to consider as you set out: like Dan Hilbert, you have to think deeply about who is most valuable, why they are valuable, and how much of your recruiting resources can be dedicated to getting them on board. More broadly, you have to monitor and improve the organizational effectiveness of your hiring practices.

We'll take these in order, first thinking about who are the most valuable employees—and therefore the most urgent candidates to attract.

Who Is Most Valuable?

Managers are commonly advised to document their staff into three performance levels, and then "love the As, improve the Bs, and get rid of the Cs."

Even among the A-level players, however, there are roles that create the most value, and when you need to allocate recruiting time and money, this is the place to start. Sure, you want everyone you hire to perform well, but your hiring practices must deliver the most critical people first. You can have the best bookkeeper in town, but if you run a landscaping business, the people who show up on a customer's lawn will have more impact on your bottom line than that excellent bookkeeper.

What differentiates you from your competition? Is it great product development or customer service or operational efficiency? Which roles create that difference? This might cut across departmental lines and often cuts across the hierarchy. A company driven by sales talent had better lay the foundation of its hiring methods with the needs and mindset of great salespeople in mind; a company that beats the competition with an attitude of customer service that cuts across departmental lines needs to understand the people at any level who improve customer service.

Michael Armano, EVP, Human Resources at Palladium Group, a professional services firm, the critical players in your organization your "dominant talent segment."

"A lot of companies apply a broad-brush brand message to recruiting, thinking they'll attract and retain almost anyone," says Armano. "It's not a good idea, because different talent segments are attracted and retained by doing very different things."

Most organizations sense who is most valuable, but this does not diminish the need for other roles. It reflects your need to focus many hiring activities around your most critical "customer segments" among candidates. Remember the welders, however, and be prepared to identify high-value employees outside of the organization chart.

For example, here are some roles in a mid-sized consumer products firm, separated into four segments, or "buckets"; note that "management" is present in most areas:

- **Brings in revenue.** Sales representative, direct marketing roles, e-commerce technical design and operation
- **Operations/saving money or time.** Finance and accounting roles, legal roles, human resources administrator, facilities manager, executive assistant, information technology specialist, and sales support
- **Supports the customer.** Customer service roles, Web site help manager, and order fulfillment
- **Creates product or service.** Product development, market research, manufacturing, and creative services

Determining the most critical positions at your organization depends on which "buckets" you've committed to create competitive advantage. If lower prices derived from efficient operations (as in a discount retailer like Best Buy) are your key business advantage, then the people in the operations/saving money or time bucket are critically important. Your company's recruitment staff should tailor its messages and activities to those people foremost. If your profits depend on selling more expensive products and services than the competitors' but with greater perceived value (as in a high-end electronics business like Bose), then roles in sales, marketing, or product development might demand the most attention.

The several key roles you identify might be quite different in temperament as well as skills. Software engineers are different from sales representatives, who are different from collection managers, who are different from service technicians. As you assemble the components of a great hiring system, the preferences of your most valuable players will help you design their experience when they come in contact with your company.

> *Build your work around your most valuable players, and make adjustments as necessary to fill less critical roles.*

In Chapters 5 to 11, you'll learn to create themes and techniques to attract and acquire most in-demand talent. You'll gain the tools to build your work around your most valuable players, and make adjustments as necessary to fill less critical roles.

The mindset of the poised worker should also inform the experience for candidates that you want to create. Her skepticism, for example, means that every interaction has to be authentic. Poised candidates take a "show-me" attitude toward phrases like "great benefits" or "leading-edge business products." Speak to their self-reliance, especially in key roles, by acknowledging that they have choices about who they work with, for how long, and why.

During this process, it's also vital to ask what qualities make someone succeed at your organization. Certainly a personal commitment to institutional goals and values is important, but a wide range of temperaments, work styles, and backgrounds can share those. Go deeper: study your most successful people and determine what they have in common. Do the managers share a common set of methods? Do they have similar work styles, or do they arrive at the same goals through different paths? Do they display similar qualities of leadership, creativity, or intellectual ability? If your most valuable people all work in one area, do they have similar skill sets?

This line of questioning can also highlight potential pitfalls such as a lack of diversity within your organization (see Chapter 11).

The following are questions for readers to ask themselves (and their employees and CEOs) as part of assessing the strength of their current hiring. You can quantify the answers with a detailed survey, or just use the questions for debate, discussion, and soul-searching.

- Do employees have the same vision of the organization as leadership?
- What percentage would recommend us as an employer to their best friend?
- How do they rate the authenticity of our "employer brand"? (See Chapter 5)
- What are the three most important reasons people work here, according to them?
- How do answers differ among our employee segments (high performers vs. average, different career levels, different departments, job titles, etc.)?
- What qualities of temperament, work habits, or values do our highest-performing employees have in common?
- Do exit interviews reveal a dominant reason for voluntary exits (other than money)?
- How strong is our quality of hire?
- What percentage of hires is rated A-level performers after one year?

Eric Winegardner, director of product adoption at Monster, notes that a painful but necessary part of self-discovery is the exit interview conducted when someone leaves for another company. "When you sit in on most exit interviews, you discover managers and human resources generalists frame the situation wrongly," Eric says. "They ask, 'What's better about where you're going than where you are? Are the benefits better . . . is the salary better . . . what about the manager, what about the office?'

"Most of the time, though, people are leaving a situation with a leap of faith that they'll be happier. It's the HR truism: people join companies but quit bosses. So I ask, 'Why did you take that leap of faith? Were you looking at job listings actively, beating down people's doors? Or did you just get a recruiter's call and suddenly started questioning your job?'

"Did she decide at one point that she just wanted to get out? Was there a time when she was at risk, and why didn't we know about it? Not everyone's as happy as you think they are, especially if you take them for granted.

MY POV

"The management of talent and human resources isn't just one thing. It's not only about learning and development. It's not about the assimilation and onboarding and bringing people into your culture. It's not solely about who you hire and how you get them and where they come from. It's not just about their performance ratings or promotions.

"It's about all of those things and a systematic approach to connecting them. So when we talk about how hiring can be strategic, we ask

- What is the business need and where's the business going?
- What are the implications of that to the talent that we have?
- What are the implications of that to the talent that we're going to need?

"When you know the answers to those, then you can ask, what levers within that system are we going to pull to sort of help the organization hit its business targets?"

—Rocky Parker, Director of Recruiting and Staffing, Nationwide Financial

"The critical question to ask in an exit interview is not 'why are you leaving?' but 'why were you looking?'"

Monitor Your Recruiting Effectiveness

We hear recruiting professionals complain that they don't have a seat at the table when it comes to the highest level of business strategy. They believe that recruiting is lumped in with all the other "soft" human resources functions and not seen as strategic. While there is some truth to this complaint—especially since recruiting is only now emerging as a mission-critical practice—we think the greater issue is money.

Any company can play with ROI models in recruiting. You can tie recruiters to different departments, or tie the department's work as a whole to the bottom line. You can measure the contribution of new employees relative to older ones.

Many organizations make a desultory stab at judging the performance of recruiting with behavioral measures like time to hire or cost per hire. Relying on one or two process metrics is better than nothing, but stopping there might divert attention from recruiting's mission to build a great company with great people.

When we talk to companies about performance measurement, we often find that the professional recruiter is not experienced in the skills required to model her business, is subject to distorting measurements, and can't measure the value her work brings to the organization—even when that value is obvious and acknowledged. What numbers could legitimately work among all these crosscurrents?

What's required here is not a single model, but a framework in which the recruiting practice can be assessed on performance (how well it provides service to its customers) and on value (how performance influences the bottom line).

However attractive your company or message, there is no substitute for good management of the recruiting function itself. Whether you are a generalist in a small company, an entrepreneur building a business, or a full-time professional recruiter, you must bring to bear the same basic rules of accountability and reality checking as you would to any other business function.

Who's Accountable?

In a well-run company, you must have a genuine business case to get the money. Recruiters who avoid making a case based on numbers share responsibility for their status. It's understandable—so many recruiters work in a world of right-brain skills: communication, organizational psychology, candidates' motivations, and personal culture . . . all that human stuff. Few have worked with numbers beyond a staff budget or company salary ranges.

Furthermore, recruiting often has a peculiar relationship to the rest of the organization. If finance produces an inaccurate balance sheet, you know whom to blame. If product development produces a product that doesn't work, well, they got it wrong. But when recruiting attracts the wrong people . . . the new hire's manager becomes accountable for their performance. If recruiting brings in an ace sales rep, the sales department cards that rep's revenue and her manager gets credit.

A classic impediment to measuring the quality of a recruiter's work is attribution. If a new hire is a star, does the recruiter get credit for finding him, or does the hiring manager, who made the final hiring decision, get the credit? If a new hire's performance improves over time, is it because she's a quick learner, or highly skilled, or because the hiring manager is a great teacher? And what credit does the recruiter get for the new hire's ability to learn? That's one of those hard-to-measure skills. How do you quantify the recruiter's contribution if she fills the company pipeline with star talent but in the profit-and-loss statements those people's contributions all get put on someone else's card?

Ultimately, those who hire have to make a case for the contribution their hiring expertise makes. It's more important to apply consistent rules for accountability than following one single formula.

Lately, recruiting has established an identity and an accountability quite separate from its human resources cousins like benefits administration, training, communication, and workplace safety. Executives who truly empower a recruiting practice assess its value according to a set of standards and goals used by every department. To provide them (and yourself) with the right information, you have to agree on three principles, based on answers to the following questions:

1. *How will you measure and benchmark recruiting?* Measure what you're doing, and you can understand what works. Benchmark hiring practices like time to fill a position and number of employees found through referral programs against industry standards and you can see progress (or lack of it). Most activities in hiring can be quantified and assigned a value.[2]

2. *How will you link recruiting metrics to enterprise metrics?* Your recruiting metrics mean little unless they have a provable effect on enterprise metrics—revenue, cost containment, strategic goals, and the like. Simply showing a decrease in, say, time to hire is one thing; linking it directly to revenue gains is more persuasive.

3. *How will you use the linkage to make decisions?* The rationale behind linking recruiting metrics and enterprise metrics must follow through to the decision-making process. For example, a decision to invest $20,000 to upgrade a corporate careers site can be modeled against metrics like the average cost of locating a candidate résumé, time to fill a position, or how many candidates sign up for your update newsletter. All can be assigned a value.

Recruiting is management, after all, and when new data come to light or the situation changes, managers have to adjust. But that's what they are paid to do. Here are the kinds of questions executive or professional recruiters ask themselves to determine the strength of the organization's recruiting practice:

- How long does it take me to fill senior positions?
- What am I paying relative to the market?

- Have I defined my core employee segment?
- How many of my core employee segment are A-level players?
- What percentage of new hires become A-level players in one year?
- Do I know what attracts my core segments—the most important players?
- How well do I persuade candidates to undergo disruption in addition to the unusual transition?
- How many of my new hires come from internal referrals?
- Am I hitting my recruitment goals in high-priority segments (functional area, diversity, core hiring segments)?

Whatever the state of your recruiting today, now is the time to move from the transactional model of filling job requisitions to a longer-term, deliberate practice. In the next chapters, we'll teach you how to formulate a program to create an authentic and attractive employer brand, and use it to bring in the best.

Review

- Moving the hiring practice from improvisation to discipline begins with a clear-eyed understanding of your situation. Determine the effectiveness of your current hiring practices, the quality of your employees, and your employees' experience at work.
- Determine which employees are most valuable based on objective criteria, aligned to business goals. Concentrate more hiring resources, and the themes of your hiring messages, on them (see Chapters 5 to 8).
- The strength of your recruiting practice must be determined now and over time by objective criteria, agreed upon in advance between executive management and recruiting/human resources staff.

Chapter 5
Employer Branding

A
t a Monster sales conference a few years back, we had lunch with a Monster customer, a human resources executive from PepsiCo we'll call Sharon. She asked the waiter for a Diet Pepsi. When told that the hotel restaurant served only served Coca-Cola, she replied brightly, "That's okay. Here's ten dollars. Your gift shop has Pepsi. Please buy me a Diet Pepsi, buy one for yourself, and keep the change. It's on my employer, PepsiCo."

"Diet Pepsi" is a product. "Pepsi" is a brand. "PepsiCo" is an *employer brand*. Sharon turned a cola-war moment into a distinct, positive impression of PepsiCo, the employer—uncompromising, inventive, generous, and fun.

A brand is more than letters on a blue can of pop. It's the full experience of the product on a user's five senses, his mind, and emotions. In the language of marketing, "Pepsi" includes all the impressions that surround the product—anticipation of enjoyment, how easy it is to find, the look of the package, the taste of Pepsi, and feelings associated with the product like "fun" and "energetic."

If all that can be evoked by the name of a carbonated beverage, how much more complex is the employer brand captured in the name of an organization? What does it say about the experience of working there? Is it fun, challenging, interesting, and well paying? Is it stressful, frustrating, or unfair? Will the employee be physically, emotionally, and financially rewarded? Is it a cool place to work? Is it successful or in decline? Are all the attributes of the employer brand clear, or are they confused, contradictory, or vague? Do prospective candidates experience a feeling of anticipation . . . or dread . . . or indifference?

An employer brand is the full physical, intellectual, and emotional experience of people who work there, and the *anticipated experience of candidates who might work there*. It is both the vision and the reality of what it means to be employed there. It is both the promise and the fulfillment of that promise. The employer brand radiating out of your organization's name inspires loyalty, productivity, and a sense of pride . . . or it doesn't.

In marketing terms, a brand's image is grounded in three dimensions:

- **Functional benefits.** What the product does, for example: "this Canon digital camera takes good pictures" and "this particular model is great for portraits, video, and long-distance shots."
- **Emotional benefits.** How a product makes the customer feel, for example: "I feel happy when I see this beautiful shot of my kids" and "I feel loving and fun when I e-mail these pictures to their grandparents."
- **Reasons to believe.** Validation of the product's claims, for example: "Canon means reliability and ease of use" and "reviewers on CNET.com rate the Canon digital camera as excellent."

A solid employer brand is grounded in the same dimensions:

- **Functional benefits.** Tangible rewards of working at the employer: salary, health care, a clean, safe workplace, and a convenient location; for example: "XYZ Co. has great compensation and has a beautiful office near my home."

- **Emotional benefits.** Intangible rewards: mission, pride, status, job satisfaction, companionship/collegiality, belonging to a "winning team," and so on; for example: "I'm proud to work for XYZ Co.—my pals and I make the best widgets in the world."
- **Reasons to believe.** Validation of the employer's claims; for example: "My friend says XYZ Co. is a great place to work" and "the local news station calls XYZ Co. a hot company for talented people."

Note that functional and emotional benefits are used for "positioning," which means defining the unique combination of attributes that define the product (or employer). XYZ Co.'s positioning says that it has a winning culture combined with strong tangible rewards, which in combination with other attributes creates a unique identity. XYZ's competitors will have different cultures, locations, compensation packages, and so on.

Branding includes deliberate messages about the company. For example, PepsiCo, which employs 153,000 employees worldwide, promotes the tag line "PepsiCo—Taste the Success!" to candidates to convey the excitement of working at this global company. On its corporate recruiting Web site, PepsiCo says its workplace experience is a combination of "Powerful Brands, Passion for Growth, Culture of Shared Principles, Commitment to Results, Ability to Make an Impact, and Quality People." At that sales meeting, Sharon embodied those qualities in her behavior.

Candidates form powerful impressions of employers based on what they see and hear. "I work for PepsiCo" means something different from "I work for Microsoft," "I work for Fox News," and "I work for the city council." The employer brands at these organizations are crafted to attract certain kinds of talent, temperament, and values in candidates. Their positioning is unique and distinctive.

Employer branding is not just an initiative of big companies, because everyone can (and does) develop a reputation. Ask a landscaper about three local lawn service companies and he'll tell you the differences among them—this one says you'll work with the best crew chiefs; that one says it pleases every customer every time, and the third one isn't much fun but pays just a little better. Those are employer brands just as real as PepsiCo's.

You have an employer brand whether you know it or not. It touches all moments of the candidate and employee experience, from the first time a candidate hears your name until the day he or she retires from your company. It's your reputation outside and inside the organization. It's there for you to neglect or manage. And it's the cornerstone of finding, hiring, and holding keepers up and down the organization. In other words, it's fundamental to all stages of the Engagement Cycle.

The idea of an employer brand has gained currency in the last few years among business leaders, but the average manager doesn't have a developed view of what it is and its importance to the organization. *The Economist* magazine found that executives defined an employer brand as the expression of a company's distinctive employment experience.[1] More than 70 percent of respondents in the United States and United Kingdom expected that developing a strong employer brand leads to employees recommending their organization to others as an attractive place to work, and also to higher employee retention.

The employer brand is an authentic description of an experience, similar to a consumer brand. It includes pay, working conditions, culture, job title, intangible rewards, and the emotional connection employees have with the organization and manager. It tells candidates who you are, what you want, and what you stand for. As a marketer attracts customers with a compelling product brand, a company attracts candidates with a compelling employer brand.

We think an employer brand is more than a one-way description of "what it's like to work there." It's a multidimensional conversation among the company's leadership, its employees, candidates in the marketplace, alumni, and even outsiders such as the press, bloggers, and anyone else who has an opinion. The employer brand includes

- The company's professional reputation
- A description of company culture
- News reports about the company, both favorable and unfavorable

- Word-of-mouth statements about the company
- A description of the company's future
- How the employer's brand compares to the competition

Beyond conversation, it's also a set of subjective candidate experiences, such as

- Applying for a job on your Web site or via e-mail
- Interviewing for a position
- Talking to employees and walking through the workplace site(s)
- Using products, services, or customer help
- The company's impact in the candidate's community

What emerges in the candidate's imagination is a fuller story than any recruiting slogan can capture: it's an experience.

This might all sound a little esoteric, but in fact it's simply recognizing reality. Candidates pay attention to an organization's reputation and compare it to other reputations. They ask employees what it's like to work there. In the quest for quality, employer branding is the foundation of attracting the right people. This is where the thought you've given to the new candidate comes together with the urgent need to bring great talent into your organization. The new candidate, as we've noted, is empowered to compare your organization to others, and he'll start with the employer brand.

Here's a typical hiring situation in which the employer brand makes a difference: A mortgage broker, already employed at a bank, gets a call from a recruiter. "Come work for this leading financial services firm and make a lot of money," says the recruiter. Instantly the mortgage broker begins to weigh the reputation of the firm against his current employer . . . are they prestigious or unknown? Are they thought of as a sweatshop or a fun place to work? Will he be proud to approach customers with that name on his business card? Does he know people at the firm, and are they happy to work there? If the answers aren't right, he might not be receptive to the recruiter's pitch.

He might even think of their advertising, charity affiliations, and location—all relevant factors in trying to judge the experience of working there.

To imagine the power of employer branding, think also of how hard it is for organizations in crisis to attract talent (except for turnaround specialists). A reputation as "a lousy place to work" is part of the death spiral that afflicts failing companies. It's a grim but true reminder that reputation matters.

People have affinities for brands. People who use Apple computers, iPods, and other devices respond to the brand's hip image. You feel different driving a BMW than a Hyundai in part because you associate yourself with the brand, and that colors your experience. Don't you respond in a similar way to the organization where you spend 40 to 60 hours a week?

Let The Cycle Be Unbroken

A break in the Engagement Cycle—that is, losing the engagement of a candidate or employee—sets you back to the beginning.

- You attract someone with great advertising *but* he has a negative interviewing experience and rejects your offer.
- You attract the wrong person *but* he comes onboard.
- You attract and acquire the right person *but* have created a false impression during the interview process—and that person leaves.
- You attract and acquire the right person, then don't advance him—he outgrows his job and the competition acquires him (and your investment in him).

The lesson: you can't run the Engagement Cycle by focusing on only one phase. A cardinal rule of branding is to maintain a consistent experience throughout the cycle.

Your employer brand becomes the theme that runs throughout the Engagement Cycle. It's a standard against which you can judge whether all the tasks around attracting, acquiring, and advancing talent are working together. If your efforts are unified by the right employer brand, you will look for the right people, create the right employment advertising, do the right networking and other outreach programs, and explain the advantages of working for you versus your competition. You'll capture the candidates who share your values and will succeed, and take a pass on candidates (even talented ones) who won't work out.

Furthermore, an authentic employment brand is a challenge to your organization's management to walk the talk—to manage daily work according to a set of values and standards that identify your company. This means employees know who they're joining, what they're expected to do, and how they will be judged.

Do you see that your employment brand is in fact the heart and soul of your company? It's really an articulation of why you exist, why you work, and why someone should work *here* and not someplace else. It's that important.

Employer by Design

You don't have to have a master's degree in marketing to see the interplay between your employment brand and your management style. You don't even have to be a big business. Consider the following true story.

We know two diners in towns nearby. The menus are the same, the prices are the same, and they even look alike.

The owner of a diner in one town has had the same waitresses for seven years. You walk in and they pour your coffee or make your tea and ask if you want the usual. The cook's been there for seven years, too. When the manager needs a new employee, he can get one through word of mouth.

The owner of the diner in another town turns over his staff every six weeks. You walk in, and nobody knows you. Everyone's learning, so the service is slow. Everyone knows they probably won't be there next season. When the owner needs a new employee, he puts a Help Wanted sign in the window.

Now, where do you want to eat? No doubt you answered the first town's diner. The diner there presents a better experience for the customers because it's a better experience for the employees. Customers enjoy themselves, and then they return.

The waitresses at this first diner tell us the owner treats the employees (and their families) like gold, like his children. He doesn't lay them off in the winter, even though it's a tourist town and he makes less money between October and May. He throws little recognition dinners for them. He goes out of his way to make them feel a little bit special. He walks around the diner and asks customers, "Is Karen treating you well? Yeah, she's the best."

MY POV
A Taste of the Real World

"San Antonio has a small-town feel when it comes to hiring, and word of mouth about our pre-graduation outreach has really helped us out.

"What do we do that's different? Here's an example: Many new nurses get on a unit and—Day One—they're assigned seven patients. They're thinking, "What the heck did I get myself into? They didn't teach me about this in school." They're not prepared for real life in the unit. We talk to nursing students a couple of semesters in advance of graduation and encourage them to join our 'externship' program. They work in nurse's aide positions, and they learn what life in the hospital is really like. It's also an opportunity for us to 'try before we buy.' We wind up converting probably 80 percent of the externs into the next level of the training program because we know them, they know us, and they've proven themselves."

—Barry Burns, Director of Human Resources,
Methodist Healthcare System, San Antonio, Texas

This small business owner has become a great employer by design. He set out to be a great employer from the beginning, maybe just as a matter of his character. The brand, in its local, intimate way, just expresses this.

Meanwhile, the owner of the diner in the second town knows he can always get *someone* to wait tables in his diner. He doesn't care whom, and it shows in his customers' experience. Maybe he doesn't have time to throw parties for his waitresses or learn their kids' names. Instead, he spends his time hiring or training new staff—over and over again. That Help Wanted sign never seems to leave his window.

Leadership and Branding

The genesis of a good employment brand starts from the top, with courageous leadership. Google gets it. They're scooping up the talent base in Silicon Valley and elsewhere. Details of their employment brand change as they grow, but the allure of working with the best, working at Google *because* you're one of the best, has been central to its employment brand from the beginning.

Southwest Airlines is another great example. Herb Kelleher's fundamental belief has been that engaged employees make happy customers, and he has been willing to break the status quo of the airline business. Southwest would "hire attitude and train skills," build a good working relationship with unions, maintain profit-sharing for employees, celebrate corporate milestones, and treat employees like family in a hundred small ways. Southwest has cut bureaucracy and honored hard work at all levels, from the boardroom to the baggage ramp. Southwest has consistently been named a *Fortune* magazine "Best Place to Work." Talk to someone who works at Southwest and he or she will rant about loving the company, even though airline work is notoriously stressful.

Nike doesn't have to maintain a state-of-the-art campus. It doesn't have to spend tens of millions a year on athletic fields, basketball and tennis courts, and driving ranges for the employees. Nike would attract a decent workforce just by its product brand alone. But Nike's leadership thinks it's a business and moral imperative to make the experience of working there something like living in a

Nike commercial, and they have had the courage to spend the money to make that a reality. It has taken some time for those measures to pay off on the company's profit-and-loss statements, but they have, and a big part of that has been the incredible engagement its employer brand has inspired.

Counter service is hard, often tedious work—but Starbucks has reinvented the role of the "barista" with its reinvention of the coffee shop. Anyone can call the help an "associate," but Starbucks has offered better benefits, a more pleasant atmosphere, and cachet that its competitors have simply lacked.

Notice a pattern here? These companies are known for shaking up their industries or even inventing entire new categories of service. Nike, Southwest, Nordstrom . . . they're all rule breakers in their industries. Diageo in Ireland, SAP in Germany, and FedEx worldwide attract the best by being distinctive. That goes for companies you have never heard of as well, because you don't have to be big to build a strong employer brand. (In fact, it's often easier for smaller, private companies to forge a distinct identity as employers, because they are more nimble and can create a local identity.)

The leadership of these companies have created their success by challenging the status quo on all fronts and seeking the highest standards of leadership, whether in product development, service delivery, or talent management. They see hiring as another opportunity to "do it better."

Bad employer branding also flows from the top, and it's easy to recognize. We know a company that's sending the right message to one of its employee groups, and the wrong message to another.

The company's corporate headquarters is in a shining glass tower rising like Oz in a beautiful landscape. You walk into a cool, bright atrium and notice the clean offices and state-of-the-art daycare facilities. Corporate managers enjoy health and fitness programs and running trails; headquarters has all the amenities you'd ever want.

Then, you visit the nearest terminal for this company—the place where the drivers work—and it's an old, dirty, cramped concrete building with dozens of dark bays and a tarmac like a greasy 10-acre griddle, and broken vending machines in dark corridors. For the driver working in that warehouse, the employment brand is no better, and probably worse, than that of the competitors'. Today, there's a shortage of 20,000 truck drivers in the United States. When workers are in desperately short supply, you cannot win if your employer brand is lousy for a critical group of your employees.

These organizations, from the small-town diner to Nike, are living examples of employer brands. To bring that statement full circle, let's add that the employees' experiences *are* the employer brands, for good or bad, brilliant or mediocre. The employer brands attract candidates (or don't) because they make an authentic, attractive statement about the meaning of work at that business.

Great employer branding is a reflection of great leadership, good management, and the hard work of getting that message out to the people who you've identified as the right candidates.

Note that these companies keep the employment brand experience consistent with the overall brand. Nike's employment brand is sporty, enthusiastic. Starbucks stores have a hundred visual, tactile, and olfactory cues that create their unique set of experiences (the ball caps and aprons matter). That small-town diner is a friendly, family-oriented place and the owner treats his staff like family.

It's up to an organization's leaders to create a great work experience out of which the employer brand is born. If working at your company is a lousy experience, you won't get off the pain train of turnover. You won't land the best talent and even when you do, you won't keep them for long. Your branding efforts will be futile. Candidates and employees know a good work experience from a bad one, and if you are not telling the truth about your organization, they'll know quickly. Most of the time, the problem is not outright lying but spin.

> *Great employer branding is a reflection of great leadership, good management, and the hard work of getting that message out to the people who you've identified as the right candidates.*

Today's candidate recognizes spin, too, because it's everywhere in the recruiting business. Think of the catch phrases you see in job ads: "we're a team," "work-life balance," and "relaxed atmosphere." What do any of those mean?

Write It Down

It is the job of senior leadership, hiring managers, and human resources professionals to articulate the employer brand and integrate it into every task in hiring. It's time to put fingers to keyboard and start writing.

When you articulate your employer brand, you improve the other components of a recruiting strategy. Employee referral programs become more effective; local media report your reputation (and, if you're a large organization, national media report it too); more of the right candidates apply. The message can be reinforced throughout the entire Engagement Cycle.

Your message has to be direct, authentic, and compelling, even if you are not fully happy with the current state of your workplace. Perhaps you aren't number one in your market, fast-paced, fun, or interesting. Perhaps your workforce isn't as engaged as you wish it were (improving your workforce is, after all, the point of this book).

Nevertheless, you must articulate an authentic message, even if it is not fully realized. That means describing the company's unique mission, its values, and its culture. If you work in a large organization, chances are the leadership has articulated a vision for that company. Usually an organization's vision is an attempt to say where it's going, or a great big ambition. Sometimes it's closer to an identity, like Nike's "Just Do It." In a smaller organization, it's more a feeling of "we stand for the following . . . ."

Let's be clear what we mean by values at an organization: they are the criteria by which all critical business decisions are made. They are statements of principle from which outcomes flow, whether those outcomes are "the highest possible profits," "a world where no child goes to bed hungry," or "beautiful landscapes."

A message about values is absolutely critical in your marketing outreach, not only so you attract people who share your values, but also to help prevent people who don't share your values from joining the organization.

And culture? Just as you already have an employer brand, whether you know it or not, you have a culture, whether it was created deliberately or "just sort of happened." Culture is the way in which people interact with each other and the organization as a whole. Culture is the outward expression of values. A conscious example of creating a culture from values can be found at women's apparel company Eileen Fisher, which made the Great Place to Work Intitute's 2007 list of great medium-size companies to work for.[3] The company states its practice as "to work as a reflection of how our clothing works, simply and in connection" and goes on to describe exactly what that principle means in terms of employees' individual growth, collaboration and teamwork, attitude, and social consciousness.[4]

Software company Intuit promotes "Operating Values" like "integrity without compromise," "seek the best," and "speak, listen and respond" that not only describe values but the behavior that is the outward expression of values.[5] That's culture.

People recognize culture, and it can be a powerful attraction to highly talented candidates. Good employer branding incorporates culture because it's one of the intangible benefits that make an impression on the poised candidate.

Here, for example, is how Monster combines statements about its mission, values, and culture to articulate its overall employer brand.

Mission: Bringing people together to advance their lives.

Values:
- Entrepreneurial passion and innovation
- Leadership
- Customer intimacy
- Fairness in all you do
- A zeal to win
- The Monster team
- Accountability, i.e., "do what you say"

cont'd on page 64

Cont'd from page 63

Description of the Culture

The culture at Monster is all about being first, being fast, and being out front. From day one you'll notice a Monster difference. You'll see people challenging themselves and questioning conventional thinking to contribute innovative ideas. You'll lead a brainstorming session, eat lunch, and play Ping-Pong in our huge Monster Den. But most of all, you'll see an entire company of people committed to owning a marketplace, making their mark, and making the most of every day.

Here's another version, from a company we admire:

*Enterprise Rent-A-Car Founding Values**

- Our brand is the most valuable thing we own.
- Personal honesty and integrity are the foundation of our success.
- Customer service is our way of life.
- Enterprise is a fun and friendly place, where teamwork rules.
- We work hard ... and we reward hard work.
- Great things happen when we listen ... to our customers and to each other.
- We strengthen our communities, one neighborhood at a time.
- Our doors are open.

*From http://aboutus.enterprise.com/what_we_believe/founding_values.html

cont'd on page 65

Cont'd from page 64

Enterprise lives by a six-point "Cultural Compass" that includes comprehensive descriptions of the employee's expected behaviors concerning operations, diversity, work/life balance, business practices, community relations and philanthropy, and government relations. For example: the Compass's true north, Operations, is the fuel that drives Enterprise. Our profitability provides us with the resources to do all that society expects of us and that we expect of ourselves: things like creating jobs, investing in growth opportunities, and investing in our communities. We have to be good business people first and foremost: we must constantly work to satisfy our customers and to treat employees with respect. We must also be superior operators and competitors; after all, our devotion to focused operations with a competitive spirit is what made us not only the largest car rental company in North America but also the best.

Furthermore, branding only matters if it reaches your target audience—so describe your employer brand for the poised worker. Since your job is to articulate the employer brand that already exists, in reality and in aspiration, start with your employees. Solicit candid input from your current workforce because, as we've seen, a large section of them are poised workers. Your current employees are the experts; if you start anywhere other than their experience, you are writing fiction.

Ask your employees these questions:

Values Questions

- What do we as an organization believe?
- How do we choose which projects get done?
- On what criteria is your performance judged?
- Are we fair?
- How do we treat customers?
- Which customers deserve the most attention?

Culture Questions

- Why are you here?
- What is unique about us?
- What is your relationship to the customer?
- Why would your customer do business with you?
- What outcomes do you want from your work?
- How do we achieve our goals?
- Describe the kind of person who succeeds here.
- What do we want people who work here to feel for this place?
- What, other than money, would tempt you to leave?
- Would you recommend this organization to a close friend?

You should also develop a more detailed list of "features and benefits" of working at your organization. These are the details that HR professionals and recruiters love to discuss, because they're more concrete than mission and culture:

- Job description
- Compensation details (salary, bonuses, hourly rate, profit sharing)
- Benefits of all kinds—medical, 401(k) and pension plans, savings
- Business line—your products and services
- Business opportunity—the upside of working for you, the chance to advance a career
- Lifestyle—"work-life balance" or "intense atmosphere;" a job's travel requirements, etc.
- Location
- Positioning in the industry (best products, "employer of choice" status)
- Community service and other outward expressions of culture
- Recognition from the outside

You don't advertise with this list because, frankly, these features and benefits play backup in the employer brand. A list is just not as compelling as a statement (or better, a narrative). The features and benefits of a job might help you close a deal with a talented individual, or tip the balance against a competitor, but they aren't effective in getting attention.

Details help, and it's important to accentuate all the positive things that go on in a company. Monster's Lori Erickson remembers that "when I took this job at Monster there were benefits we offer that I didn't even know about. We have an adoption assistance program and nursing rooms for new mothers in every single facility across the United States. We have a work-life person whose sole job is to put programs in place that make it easier for employees to balance the challenges of having a life and a job. We had to learn to push that message into the recruiting story."

Your first attempt to define an employer brand doesn't have to be perfect, but it does have to satisfy a few rules:

- **Is it authentic?** Does your statement reflect reality? Do employees recognize the values and the culture you describe?
- **Is it unique?** Would an employee know that this describes your organization and not a similar one?
- **Is it compelling?** Docs it demand action? Does it describe the meaning of working at your organization?
- **Is it relevant?** Is your statement meaningful to the people you're trying to attract?
- **Does It describe un experience?** As far as candidates, potential candidates, and employees are concerned, your employer brand is an experience. It's not a slogan, and it's not a logo, and it's not a press release. It's the good or bad deal of investing another day of their one-and-only lives in your organization.

The answers to each of these questions must be yes, because otherwise you'll miss your audience. Rigorous questioning of the statement worked for Laura Stanley, who leads the Talent Acquisition and Employment Branding team at EarthLink in Atlanta. She started her work with a reality check: "When I joined, the first thing I did was to ask my team, 'Okay, why do people join, and

One More Reason to Write Your Story

A compelling story doesn't just attract talent, it begins the selection process by separating those who find your employer brand attractive from those who don't. A "one-size-fits-all" vision leads to mediocre candidate pools. Anybody can be attracted to statements like "you'll work with great people and enjoy the challenge." But you want people who resonate with your authentic brand identity and employer brand to come knocking.

One problem with attracting a huge number of candidates (because you want to appeal to so many in hopes of picking out the best) is that you burden yourself with a much larger sorting process than necessary.

A well-articulated employer brand helps avoid false starts. We know some great people who have come to Monster and failed. When that happened, we always wondered, did they fail because of their skills or because their values were misaligned to the company? Think of great mismatches in business—for example, John Sculley at Apple and Michael Ovitz at Disney—they had considerable skills, they clearly could succeed in the roles they had, but they were a serious mismatch with the companies they were supposed to lead.

Your employer brand should *attract* the people you really want (the ones who will fit) and *discourage* the people who won't work out . . . especially the qualified candidates who ultimately won't fit your culture.

why do people not join, this company? What are our brand attributes? Why does the top talent come here to EarthLink? What does the organization need to look like in terms of our longer-term objectives—10 years out—or five years out—2010, 2009?' Through our research we've found that it's really important that you articulate pretty clearly what they're going to get when they come, and also what they've got to give, too, and to make sure that we're attracting the right people in the right jobs at the right time."

The Authenticity Check

Ask yourself (and your employees) the following questions. Then tell your CEO the answers.

- Do employees have the same vision of our employer brand as leadership?
- Do they believe the value claims of the employer brand?
- What do they think about the presentation of the employer brand?
- How do they rate the authenticity of our employer brand message?
- What about working here is most important to employees?
- Can I segment the answers (by manager's rating, seniority, tenure, etc.)?
- What details do long-term employees value most?
- What details do short-term employees value most?

It's Not Even About Your Products

Your products and services are important attributes of your employer brand, but they are not its heart and soul. Great organizations outlast their first products and their original businesses but preserve their established values. We've cited a few brands like Nike, whose products are closely aligned with their employer brand, but it's not about the sneakers—if Nike went into the automobile business, they'd design a car that was unmistakably a Nike car.

Turnaround stories provide insight to this, because rescuing an organization in trouble inevitably poses choices of what to keep and what to discard. The following is a well-known example.

IBM was in trouble in the early 1990s. The business practices, technical innovation, and branding that had made it an exemplar of a great company just a decade earlier had been bypassed by the rise of new technologies and new

Analysis: Employer Brand Delivery

A survey of current employees like the one suggested on page 69 can tell you whether your employer brand is both relevant and authentic—in short, whether you're delivering on your brand promise. When you have survey results, map them in a standard grid as we've done below, in which the vertical axis states the importance of certain brand attributes to your current employees and the horizontal axis states how well the organization delivers those.

Brand attributes important to employees (Less important → Most important)	**I** Competitive salary Pride in the Organization Competitive benefits	**II** Fun place to work Team atmosphere "Management cares about me personally." Ability to do great work
	III Cool technology Convenient location	**IV** Focused on customers

Organization's delivery of brand attributes
Weak ⟶ Strong

In an organization with a highly relevant and authentic employer brand, quadrant II is full of attributes that matter to employees, and that the organization provides and features in its brand. Attributes in quadrant I are risk factors, because they mean the organization isn't providing what matters. Attributes in quadrant III are relatively unimportant to hiring,

cont'd on page 71

Cont'd from page 70

and attributes in quadrant IV represent a disconnect between employees and brand attributes. For example, the organization profiled here has succeeded to create a positive culture based on the statements in quadrant II; it is at risk of losing people or not recruiting keepers because of pay and benefit differences in quadrant I.

Great questions come from this type of analysis: Must the company pay more to get great talent, or are people working for a little less because the culture is so good? The brand's focus on customers doesn't seem to matter a lot to employees. Why? Is that irrelevant as a selling point to candidates? Why is "cool technology" not important to employees

customer demands. Endless layers of management made it a slow-moving giant, overcome by smaller, faster competitors. A new leader, Lou Gerstner, turned the company around by focusing on customer needs, "solutions" rather than just new technology, and a consulting model that recognized that the application of technology to individual business problems was more important to customers than bells and whistles in a computer operating system.

Gerstner also deconstructed much of the organization, eliminated whole layers of management, and in many small and large ways altered the blue-suit image of the IBM employee. Eventually, the company got out of the PC business altogether.

What did not change was the essential value that IBM would deliver information technology (and by extension, the ability to use it) to solve very large business problems. Gerstner also reestablished IBM's reputation as an employer that hired an elite candidate and held employees to high standards. IBM had seen some of that reputation slide during its decline, and Gerstner rightly saw that, in a service business, the reputation of your employees for excellence is a critical business advantage—maybe the only business advantage that matters.

The importance of values to an employer brand is starkly evident in the frequently repeated story of acquisitions: A good company is acquired, then forced to change its culture to that of the new parent company. You know what happens next—the best people leave, saying, "It's just not the same around here." One key to the success of Cisco Systems' company acquisition strategy has been its ability to cushion the culture shock employees experience when a new parent company takes over. Cisco acquisition specialists say they focus on people first and products second. They treat new employees with respect in a hundred ways, like having new job titles, business cards, and pay packages ready on the day of the acquisition. They look for companies with a culture of empowerment similar to Cisco's, so the change will be less dramatic. Employees who are used to speaking their minds or taking initiative are encouraged to continue those behaviors (that is, after all, how they invented products that attracted Cisco in the first place). Turnover at the acquired companies following acquisition is as low as 1 percent.[6]

Be a Magnet Employer

Rob O'Keefe of recruitment advertising firm TMP Worldwide Advertising and Communications discussed the term "magnet employer" in a discussion of employer branding:

> A magnet employer is one that everyone wants to work for; an organization in which leadership, employees, and culture are completely aligned. They have achieved wholehearted agreement around what the organization does, how it does it, and why.
>
> When an organization becomes a magnet employer, the right people hold the organization in esteem, aspire to be part of the organization, and therefore, negate the need for the organization to engage in lead-generation activities. These strategies are instead replaced by pure brand, public relations, and internal communications efforts.

It's an ideal state to aim for, and one that requires much more than just good branding, but becoming a "magnet employer" is the goal of all these efforts. Articulating an employer brand in order to attract better candidates is a core tactic. You acquire those candidates by living the brand authentically, confirming your brand promise. Later, as employees, those talented people advance in their careers and advance the mission of the organization.

But that's getting ahead of the process; the next step (you'll learn about it in Chapter 6) is to develop the messages of your employer brand and deliver it to the best candidates.

Review

- You have an employer brand now; whether it is desirable, authentic, and under your control are the issues you must face in recruiting.
- A strong employer brand requires alignment with leadership, because it starts at the top.
- Articulate your brand based on core truths about your organization.
- An employer brand focuses on values and culture, not products or services.
- The best employer brands are based on living the brand message—they appear in the everyday work of the employees and the values of the organization.

Chapter 6

Getting to Know You

In the movie *Camelot*, King Arthur decides to assemble the greatest knights in the world in a chivalrous society. He releases dozens of carrier pigeons from his castle, each bearing an invitation to a noble hero to join him at the round table. In France, Lancelot reads the invitation and bursts into song (okay, this is a musical, after all). The world's greatest knight will accept Arthur's offer and go to Camelot.

Media technology has matured since AD 500, and you can probably give the pigeons a pass, but when you're looking for a Lancelot, you've got to use every communication you can, from advertising to the corporate Web site to word of mouth.

In this game of attraction, the poised mindset is your ally, because even the happily employed are receptive to your message. You can build a set of employer brand impressions over the long term and over time create a large audience of talented people who are interested in joining your organization.

Awareness

At this point, you've articulated the qualities of your employer brand, and so you have the beginning of a message. To attract the right people, you have to decide who they are, where they are, and how they will encounter your message. Kicking off the Engagement Cycle, you first have to get the attention of candidates and your own employees (because, as we'll see, they're part of your attraction strategy). If you understand them well enough, candidates will be attracted to you and want to take the next step.

Attraction begins with awareness: candidates have to know your name and at least one thing about you that grabs their interest. Right away, you're in danger of disappearing into the shower of advertisements and information that bombards the average person more or less constantly. Estimates of how much advertising consumers see vary widely, from 250 to 3,000 messages a day, but even if you measure to the subset of employment messages, the number is large. Every classified ad, every Web site with a careers link, and every billboard advertising a local business competes with you for a moment of candidate attention.

Those messages compete not only with each other but also with a constant stream of noncommercial demands, from the ringing cell phone to the coworker's interruption to the boyfriend's smile. Suffice to say, nobody will pay attention to your message without a good reason. (It's appropriate that we say "pay" attention since, like money, it is valuable, personal, and always in short supply!)

Every impression matters if you're going to turn awareness into attraction. First encounters with your employer brand might be decisive. Will prospective candidates want a second impression? A third? Those touch points will be moments when your employer brand is either confirmed or contradicted. Every one of them has to reinforce the central themes of your employer brand. Effective touch points work on the emotions first and the intellect second. Effective touch points project your unique attributes consistently.

Rocky Parker, associate vice president at Nationwide, discovered that putting the key attributes of working at Nationwide before even the company name had the right effect:

> For job fairs, we printed a million brochures that talk about personality. They're not the traditional financial-services-blue brochures you see in every bank and at every job fair. They don't even say Nationwide on the front; just "Personality." Inside, they say, "We look for people who breathe life and energy into their work every day."
>
> Our brochure features people talking about their passions, their commitment, connection, and leadership, and some other characteristics that we believe are important. All of our job fair displays and all of our booths and all of our handout material and all of the job descriptions and all the online job listings—all of them follow this brand message. We even changed the look of our office interview space, which now looks as if you walked into the brochure.

The Nationwide employer brand in Rocky's brochure becomes, in short, associated with its values.

The Candidate Experience

Consider the experience of applicants when they go on interviews. Many organizations treat them this way:

The applicants wait at the reception desk, and wait, and wait. Nobody offers them coffee or directions to the bathroom. Then they are led into a room decorated with nothing more than Occupational Safety and Health Administration (OSHA) and Equal Employment Opportunity Commission (EEOC) posters. They have to cram themselves into one of those little school desks and fill in a form. Then they wait again. Eventually they are taken into the darkest room in the building where an HR person grills them. Then (sometimes) a manager comes in and the candidate talks about herself for 10 minutes. Then she's told the interview is over and "we'll call you."

When we ask if this sequence is familiar to hiring managers and HR recruiters—candid ones—about 90 percent of the people in the room raise their hands. It's unbelievable.

The message they're sending is, "we don't care." Do you think a marketer would bring customers in to try a product and treat them like that?

How about this instead? People are invited to an airy and bright room with tables, comfortable chairs, and a couch. You have a video playing about the company, fresh coffee and bottled water, and recruiting literature about the company on the table. An employee stops by to talk about her fantastic experience at the company. If the candidates have to fill out an application, someone is available to help. Then they are invited to an office where they get a respectful, professional interview with trained people. They meet a prepared manager who asks relevant questions. At the end of the interview, they are told they will receive a follow-up call within a week—and they do.

That's treating a candidate like a customer.

Robert Crowder, former director of diversity recruiting at The Hartford and now at Aetna, observes that messages are sent minute by minute through the entire recruiting process. He says:

> Every touch point in which people encounter us is going to speak to how credible that brand is, from how soon somebody returns a phone call to how we wind up denying a candidate if they're not appropriate for the role. How do we behave when they walk in the door? When they're sitting in the conference room? How do we interact with each other in front of a candidate? These behaviors say whether or not The Hartford is a credible and believable brand.

To candidates, your behavior through the recruiting process *becomes* your employer brand. That's true before they set foot in the door. Let's say your company culture and employer brand emphasize respect for the customer. Since the

Marketing Shorthand

A marketer asks:

- Who is my target audience, and what do they want?
- What channels do I use to reach each group of customers?
- What is my product offering?
- What is the "customer experience" of candidates and employees?
- How does it differ from my competitors' offering?
- How do I articulate and leverage my brand attributes?
- How do I shore up the gap between a customer's desire and what I can offer?

A hiring manager *should* ask:

- Who are my target candidates, and what do they want?
- Where will I reach the most target candidates, and the fewest unqualified applicants?
- What am I offering them?
- What's the candidate's/applicant's experience?
- How do I differ from my competitors for talent?
- How do I articulate and leverage my employer brand?

candidates are the hiring manager's customers, every official touch point must emphasize respect for their time, their intelligence, and their value. Here's how that might play out:

- Every job application is acknowledged (this can be a simple auto-notification stating that the application arrived safely).

- Candidates who don't make the first cut are notified quickly and unambiguously, and thanked for their interest. The door is left open for possible future work.
- Candidates who might be appropriate for other roles in the organization are quickly notified of that possibility. For example, they might be told that their application will be directed to another department for possible future opportunities.
- Candidates who are qualified are contacted quickly, even if it's just to notify them that they are under consideration.
- Candidates who are hot prospects—clearly qualified for key roles—are notified within two days.

Everyone, Even the Also-Rans

As we write this, we can hear moans from human resources and recruiting staff everywhere: "I'm overwhelmed with inappropriate applications!" Sorting out the unqualified from the qualified takes work, but that doesn't absolve the manager from keeping the promise of respect for the customers. Simple, automated acknowledgments are sufficient to tell all candidates that their applications have been received.

There is relief from the pain of too many applicants. Technology helps, from simple database programs to advanced enterprise software (the latter for those large organizations that can justify the expense). Search engines are getting better, and experienced recruiters have become adept at sorting through applications and résumés. This begins with a clear and open-minded understanding of the people who will fit your organization.

You can even align your employer brand to aid the sorting-out process. Here's how Home Depot does it, according to Caroline Brown, Home Depot's senior manager of employment marketing:

> A lot of people think it's really fun to shop here, so it would be fun to work here. While it is fun to work at a Home Depot, it's also very challenging. We have to make sure that we're bringing in people who are up for the challenge

and who are good at customer service. One of the things that we've done is create a short video—it's called *The Realistic Shop Preview*—that shows the high points of the job and also shows the really tough parts. We host it online, and it encourages people to self-select out before they even bother applying.

Even candidates you don't hire form an impression of your organization, and if you treat them right, they can become a source of potential candidates as well. Lisa Calicchio, director of recruiting pharmaceutical teams at Johnson & Johnson, believes this and works to make every interaction a positive one. If you think you get a lot of not-quite-qualified candidates, look into Lisa's world:

> We get a million applications a year, so lots more people *don't* get hired by Johnson & Johnson than do get hired. The people who don't get hired are voices that we have to be mindful of, because people talk about their experiences. And people are quicker to talk about negative experiences than positive ones. Every candidate needs a certain amount of attention. We're not perfect, but the basic tenets of courtesy, respect, and follow-up should apply to everybody.

To know whether your hiring process authentically showcases your employment brand, get feedback at every stage of the process—when people apply, when you screen applications, and when they interview on the phone or later. You don't need to hire a consulting company to do this; instead, create a quick online survey (or question-and-answer session at the end of the job interview) and ask questions like

- Did you hear from us quickly?
- Were you treated with respect?
- What impression of the organization did you get from your visit to our Web site or office?
- Were the people you met prepared to tell you about the company and to interview you well?
- Based on your experience, would you apply for positions in the future?

MY POV

"Branding can succeed quietly. I know a company that's under the radar of most recruiters, but candidates tell me about it nonstop. Everybody with an insider's knowledge in high tech wants to work there. They're a solid organization where talent can find stability, yet they are very entrepreneurial in running their product lines. They have low turnover, and as a recruiter I get very few inquiries of current employees, because once people get in they tend to stay. Employees speak with admiration about the company. They understand the profit and loss statements—nothing hidden there. They are always jazzed about the stock price. And when you talk to any one of them—even though they work long hours—every single one has a very positive attitude. I have yet to meet one unhappy employee from this company."

—*Kristin Motta, Director of Staffing and Search, CM Access*

Most hiring organizations treat applications as a one-time event, and when they say "we'll keep your résumé on file" even the promising candidate knows she's unlikely to hear from them ever again. "We need to fill this position," implies the company, "and you're either in or you're out." That's a lost opportunity.

Let's say your business is accounting, and you're looking for auditors with five years' experience. A good candidate comes in but he's only got two years' experience. You could send him away forever with a "flush card" ("thanks for applying, blah, blah ...") or you could tell him that he's not quite ready and then ask him to subscribe to your candidate newsletter. Once a quarter, you send him and other promising auditors a newsletter with notes about what's going on in your firm. You add content that helps them learn and grow. You throw in tips written by your current auditors; maybe a portrait of a star auditor, showing her career path. Three years later, when that candidate is ready, he's predisposed to pick your company. That wasn't so hard, was it?

Companies with strong hiring practices like Accenture, Deloitte, and Siemens UK practice this long-term connection with candidates internationally, thus engaging a group of "might-someday-be-right" candidates who have already expressed interest.

Customizing Your Message

Your outreach in media is meant to inspire the right "in-reach" of prospective candidates. You want the most appropriate people approaching you, and the least-qualified candidates to stay away. That means you have to drive your employer brand into your job advertising and even into your job descriptions.

Define the persons you want to respond. In marketing terms, this is called "segmentation"—the practice of customizing critical brand messages to the unique desires or needs of a segment of your customer base so you can make the most of advertising and marketing budgets.

Note: Most product advertising is not meant to turn potential customers away, while employment marketing does strive to help nonqualified people discern that they should not apply. In this way, it's more like the marketing that colleges do to attract qualified applicants. Segmentation is practiced everywhere in advertising. For example, luxury cars and high-end financial services run commercials during golf championships, whose viewers tend to be more affluent, while football broadcasts have more soda and beer commercials.

Nike presented "Just Do It" in 1989 to its core customer segments—runners and basketball players—with a promise of performance and style. Michael Jordan personified that promise; Air Jordan basketball shoes were a technological and style innovation. Through the years, Nike customized the core message so pervasively that it could enter new market segments with a complete and relevant brand promise.

To-Do List

Ask these questions about the quality of your messages. Survey your potential candidates on the same questions.

- How long does it take me to fill senior positions?
- What am I paying relative to the market?
- Have I defined my core employee segment?
- How many of my core employee segment are A-level players?
- What percentage of new hires become A-level players in one year?
- Do I know what attracts my core segments—the most important players?
- How well do I persuade candidates to undergo disruption in addition to the unusual transition?
- How many of my new hires come from internal referrals?
- Am I hitting my recruitment goals in high-priority segments (functional area, diversity, core hiring segments)?

Back then, Nike wasn't even in the golf business, and now they're one of the top golf club manufacturers in the world. As a group, golfers are always looking for just a little better performance, and underneath "Just Do It" Nike created a message to golfers about technology leading to better performance. Nike's golf marketing featured Tiger Woods, who symbolized vitality, power, and skill beyond excellence, and the company associated its golf technology with his performance. They also created a stylish new look in golf clothes with Woods that is a signature Nike branding move. (Notice the subtle change in shape of the caps tour pros wear—that started with Woods and Nike.)

Whether it's basketball, golf, or street sneakers, Nike wants the customer for whom performance and style are more important than a low price. Nike focuses on the A-level customers: loyal, dedicated, and attached to the brand in whatever sport they love. That's the "Just Do It" message. For golfers, the message was adapted to emphasize technology. The result: a new segment of customers who feel that Nike knows what they want and pay Nike more—a lot more—for their athletic apparel.

Similarly, your communication has to begin with your central employer brand, and then be customized for the candidate who shares your values, mission, and work style. For example, if great customer service is a core value, and if your employer brand emphasizes the satisfaction of pleasing customers, you will frame that differently for each segment of your workforce, thus:

- *Customer service.* "Be the person our customers meet—embody our values to the most important people."
- *Manufacturing.* "We'll empower you to put the customer first, because we think they deserve Six Sigma quality."
- *Information technology.* "You make it possible for employees to delight our customers with fast, accurate service."
- *Human resources administration.* "Well-served employees serve customers well."

After you have established the common denominators that make individuals successful, go on to communicate the employment experience on a personal level. In the words of Rob O'Keefe of recruitment advertising firm TMP Worldwide Advertising and Communications: "Understand the group, but market to the individual. . . . Ultimately, a successful employer brand needs to be understood from the personal level in order to have any relevance or emotional context."

You won't find the single, magical advertising line that will attract everyone you need without further effort. You can, however, build a disciplined chain of communications and experiences that includes this set of action steps in your communications:

- Learn different attractions for different occupations and skill sets.
- Understand demographic and psychographic segmentation issues like diversity and inclusion, generational and life stage demands.
- Separate candidate attributes (values as well as skills and experience) into must-haves and nice-to-haves.
- Write job descriptions that inspire, challenge, and inform candidates, to attract high achievers.
- Highlight critical but hard-to-measure skills like judgment and leadership in all recruiting.
- Emphasize the intangible as well as tangible benefits of working in your organization.

Let's walk through the application of these steps.

Learn Different Attractions for Different Occupations and Skill Sets

Some recruiters, and many hiring managers, rely on generalizations about what employees want, but they don't ask employees themselves what they want. However well intended, human resources is operating in its particular corner of the company and can't be expected to fully understand the values, pressures, and priorities of people who work in other disciplines. You need a well-constructed survey, or even a fair amount of asking, to teach you what matters to your best employees (besides pay).

A large survey will still give you generalizations ("technical people tend to want this . . .") but these have some meaning, because each group faces a similar environment. For example, all your customer service representatives do similar tasks, have similar interactions with customers, and share a particular manager. The spirit in the department might be "do whatever it takes to satisfy the customer," and the manager is empowered to back that promise up with action. That becomes part of your message to prospective customer service reps.

Another example: sales representatives love to win. But language about winning appears in every sales recruiting message we've seen. What else might distinguish your company? If you introduce new products or services frequently, you can build a message around variety, novelty, and reselling an existing customer. A sales rep who likes new products is more likely to prosper at your shop.

Groups are the first step, but you attract people one at a time, so you have to go deeper into the mindset of your best employees, and to do that, you have to do the following:

Understand Demographic and Psychographic Segmentation Issues Like Diversity and Inclusion, Generational and Life Stage Demands

Does everyone at your company have the same needs, attitudes, and desires? No. Then why do the recruiting messages sound the same? People are different; you distinguish yourself from your competitors by treating candidates as individuals.

How will you discover what matters to these various cohorts? By talking to your current employees, candidates, and potential candidates. If your job posting says "senior position with flexible schedule," you'll get a different group applying than a posting titled "top technology for high-energy Web mavens." That's not to say you won't find a great 60-year-old candidate for the second position, but she will select herself based on the description.

As a simple example, let's consider the broad generational differences discussed in Chapter 2: we've seen that both the oldest and youngest cohorts in today's workforce (baby boomers and Generation Yers) want to find meaning at work and a sense that their contribution matters. They arrive at this common desire for different reasons: More financially settled boomers have worked a long time for money and later in their careers want to make an impact. Younger workers have fewer financial obligations and seek reward both in their ideals and in building a track record.

The generation in between, Generation X, doesn't necessarily have less investment as individuals in meaningful work, but as a group they tend to focus more on career building and job security issues. As a group, they have younger children than the boomers and more pressing financial responsibilities than the Millennials.

These differences have practical implications for recruiting strategy. You target each group through different communication channels—for example, advertising on Web sites that appeal to different audiences. For the same reason, you will emphasize different aspects of your employer brand. Boomers want more flexibility; you might mention that your organization encourages telecommuting. Generation Y candidates, as a group, are keenly interested in personal learning and growth, and so you might craft a message that people in your organization are expected to keep learning (especially keeping up with technology).

Hiring managers can take a simple lesson as well from good marketing and advertising: deliver your message with a face, voice, and language that encourages your target audience to identify with your organization. If you're seeking high-energy, entry-level people for your sales staff, talk to a few of those people in your organization when crafting your message. Ask, "What matters to you in this job?" Adjust your message accordingly. And then make sure that candidates who interview get a chance to meet people like themselves in the process (more on this in Chapters 8 and 11).

Be a glutton for knowledge of your current and potential workforce and the tangible and intangible benefits that attract them. Greta Roberts and Lori Moffatt of Target Teams, Inc. found that just highlighting an intangible benefit (training) improved the quality of candidates and employees. Greta tells the story:

> We worked with a financial services company whose job ads would attract entry-level people. They would come into the position and then sit through 8 to 12 weeks' worth of training and then would fail their exams. The attrition rate was extraordinarily high. They thought it was just the price they paid for rigorous training.

Guess what? Their job descriptions didn't mention the rigorous training, so they attracted the wrong candidates. There's actually a set of people for whom training is a huge motivator. They live for that. We changed the ads to read, 'We're going to give you free training. We're going to certify you. You're going to learn all about the financial services industry from one of its leading organizations.'

The quality of people answering their ads changed. Their attrition rate dropped. More people got certified. All they had to do was appeal to candidates who saw training as a perk, not a trial.

Separate Candidate Attributes (Values as Well as Skills and Experience) into Must-Haves and Nice-to-Haves

We noticed a trend in the last few years toward hyperspecific job descriptions, with more and more detail about the skills and experience required of the perfect candidate. Job seekers fretted that every job ad was written for "SuperCandidate."

In fact, some attributes are always more important than others. When defining segments of candidates to approach, rank a job's skills and experience into must-haves and nice-to-haves. This compels the hiring manager to consider in advance the choices that he will have to make later anyway. It also reflects the reality of a job. If you're in manufacturing, "Quality First" means just that, not "Quality First, but sometimes tied with Efficiency and Innovation."

When you go through the same exercise-defining values and attitudes of the perfect candidate, your choices create a richer portrait of the ideal worker.

At advertising firm Saatchi & Saatchi, Worldwide Human Interest Director Milano Reyna describes how their description flowed from the mission of the company. He says:

Our dream is to be revered as a hothouse for world-changing ideas that create sustainable growth for our clients. What kind of person do we hire to live that dream? We need dreamers. They have to be team players, because that's how we work. They have to be connected—meaning they know about the mobile world, the Web world, and other cultures. They have to connect us to other talented people. You won't be happy here if you prefer working in a cocoon. They have to be provocative, meaning can they hold someone's attention with an idea. That's crucial for media work. They have to be courageous, so they can do really creative work without waiting for approval. They have to be transformational. Around here you've got to make things happen.

These words define values, attitudes, and even temperament: dreamers, team players, connected, provocative, courageous, and transformational. Other positive qualities such as steadiness, thoroughness, broad curiosity, and a desire to serve others aren't even on the list, because while they might be nice to have, and even necessary in other businesses, they aren't what drives success in these positions.

The qualities were not *imposed on* the best people at Saatchi & Saatchi; they were *discovered in* the best people there. The big step Milano made after realizing those qualities made a successful employee was actually requiring it of new hires.

Note also that Milano connects relevant outcomes to personal qualities. "Transformative" might be a character trait, but the outcome is that the person can "make things happen." "Provocative" isn't just an attitude, it means "holding someone's attention with an idea."

Does that sound like your job descriptions? If not, you need to take the next step.

Write Job Descriptions that Inspire, Challenge, and Inform High Achievers

Better-written but still traditional job descriptions focus on achievement, that is, the outcomes expected of the skills and responsibilities they describe. This is fine as far as it goes, but high achievers are jealously guarded by their employers (you guard your high achievers, don't you?). These people need to be inspired to respond. They like challenge, and you need to offer it. They also need more information than average candidates.

Job descriptions, classified ads, and online postings are advertising. There's good advertising and bad advertising, and as consumers, we respond to both. But why would you invest in media to attract your most important asset, and then do it in a pedestrian, ordinary way like all your competitors?

Understand what makes you different. Get marketing staff to help you say it.

In the early days of Monster we would clip two or three weeks' worth of ads for a specific job out of the newspapers. They all said the same things: "we offer competitive pay, excellent benefits, and an opportunity to advance." But they were indistinguishable from one another and thus, didn't inspire a response from selective candidates.

If you want help with the language needed to grab the interest of a high achiever, ask yourself or your recruiters how they close the employment decision with top-quality candidates. They can tell you why people are applying and why they aren't. They can tell you the different needs of someone who's applying for a sales job versus an IT person, and what people do or don't like about how you describe your jobs and your culture—because they are having those conversations, every day.

Exercise: Standing Out from the Crowd

Take your job posting and do an online search and find 10 others for the same position. Print them without the company names, then post them on a wall and see if you stand out. And if you don't, use the techniques in this chapter to improve your message.

Exercise: Job Description Cheat Sheet

If you have trouble getting started, try rewriting a typical job ad along the following lines:

- Start with your employer brand.
- Identify outcomes, not just skills.
- Avoid generic phrases and claims.
- Identify qualities that fulfill your values.
- Use intangible benefits to get responses from the right people.
- Set *specific* expectations—criteria on which performance will be judged.
- Cut back on "requirements" until you know each is critical.
- Require proof of candidate's claims: requirements can say "measurable increase in customer satisfaction" or "proven sales growth overseas."

Highlight Critical but Hard-to-Measure Skills Like Judgment and Leadership

If two candidates have the same skills, and both seem like a good fit with your organization, how do you decide which to hire? You look for the intangible qualities that make all the difference in performance such as leadership, judgment, wisdom, courage, curiosity, empathy, audacity, focus, drive, ambition, and other qualities that distinguish the successful from the unsuccessful in your shop. If you're good at interviewing, you probe both candidates for those qualities, and then confirm them with references.

Why not present those qualities right up front, in your job descriptions and your job advertising? Wegmans, the supermarket chain that perennially wins "Best Place to Work" honors, is a superb example of leading with the qualities that create success within its customer-obsessed culture. Read a job posting for a Wegmans' pharmacy manager, and you see every bullet point emphasize customer satisfaction, customer delight, and customer obsession. Typical phrases:

- Uses judgment to provide incredible customer service and finds ways to say "yes"
- Recognizes customer attitudes, builds relationships with customers, and develops a substantial customer base
- Utilizes differences to provide incredible services and implement unique service features for customers

Wegmans already knows it will hire a qualified pharmacist (and states at the bottom of the ad that, by the way, the candidate must be a graduate from a school of pharmacy); it uses the job description to highlight what really matters in the job.

Most job postings will talk about what a candidate *can* do. Very few reflect what a candidate *will* do. Wegmans sets very clear expectations of people working in their pharmacy: solve customer problems; delight customers. When you think of it, the whole purpose of the job interview is to separate the "can do" from the "will do," that is, separate potential from actual behavior on the job. If you're clear about expectations up front, you'll have better outcomes later (more on this in Chapter 8).

Making employer brand messages relevant to particular types of candidates is time-consuming work. It means stepping out of the comfort zone for most managers. It's multidimensional, and many of the dimensions are difficult to quantify (what's your score on empathy?) It also has the benefit of making you think, or rethink, the actual criteria for success in a job, and like good advertising, your brand and your job positions will bring in more appropriate people.

Emphasize the Intangible as Well as Tangible Benefits of Working in Your Organization

Hiring managers and recruiters might assume that pay and benefits are the only important criteria for candidates to become interested in a job; that's a flawed assumption. In its HR practice, McKinsey & Co. discovered a significant disconnect between traditional HR focus on tangible benefits (compensation, job security, career growth) versus the candidate's focus on intangible benefits like challenge, autonomy, a sense of fun or pride, work-life balance, and other factors. The authors of a 2005 survey wrote:

> Traditional recruiting focuses on functional employment benefits, such as job security; opportunities for creativity and individual growth; and compensation. But an employer's intangible, emotional associations—'it's fun to work at this company,' 'we have a passionate and intelligent culture,' and 'there is a strong team feeling here'—are just as important to recruits as similar associations with branded consumer goods are to potential buyers.[1]

A candidate will focus on compensation if there is no other difference between prospective employers. Moreover, you often have more flexibility to offer different intangible benefits to candidates according to their preferences, as opposed to offering them different tangible benefits such as health plans.

Valero, the huge energy company, emphasizes pride in its recruiting—"Pride in our company. Pride in our jobs. And pride in our communities." That succinct message focuses on the most intangible benefit—a feeling—and goes on to state that pride is one reason people feel good about working at Valero. How intangible is that? How important is that?

Review

- Attraction begins with awareness; you have to rise above the noise of everyday advertising messages.
- The experience of all candidates, not just successful ones, is relevant to recruiting.
- Candidate feedback is an important gut check of your marketing.
- An effective marketing message is customized to your employer brand and to the particular candidate(s) you wish to attract.
- Job ads and job descriptions must merge the employer brand message with tangible and intangible benefits that are relevant to the best candidates.

Chapter 7

Send Them a Message

A résumé comes across your screen, and the person seeking the job looks fantastic. The problem is, you don't have a position that's right for him. So it's on to the next résumé.

Six months from now, however, you are going to need that person. How about starting a conversation with him now? How about giving him time to know and trust your employer brand? Six months from now, when you and your competitors are trying to hire him, whom do you think he'll remember?

Terry Frugoli, a recruiter at Microsoft, knows the value of building a full network of relationships with candidates at all levels. "One of my counterparts up in Redmond asked me to attend an off-site job fair for sales and marketing candidates," recalls Terry, who lives in San Francisco. "Even though most of the candidates were people that I wouldn't normally be talking to because I'm in a technical field, I went to the job fair."

"Why? Well, God only knows when the business will change and they'll say 'Terry, you've got to hire sales and marketing people now.' If I've stored up 50, 60, or 100 sales and marketing candidates, I have people to contact. If I've just set up a good relationship with each—even a five-minute call—then when I get back in touch it's not, 'Well, Terry, I don't have time to talk to you.' It's, 'Gosh, it's good to hear from you. You know, I'm really happy at what I'm doing, but you know what?—I know a couple of friends that are really good . . .' or, 'I'd be very interested in speaking with you about an opportunity with Microsoft.'"

If you're hiring, you're in the relationship-building business. Up to now, you've thought about how to differentiate your employer brand from the crowd. If you've done the work of Chapter 6, and you know that your job descriptions reflect your unique promise, you're ready. Now it's a matter of applying your messages to the channels that will reach your target audience in the most effective way. Start close to home, with the recruiting section of your own Web site.

Your Recruiting Web Site

The "careers" section of your Web site should reflect your culture, your values, and your opportunities. Although that sounds obvious, in the real world we're often startled by how generic, perfunctory, and, frankly, boring careers areas appear. Sometimes it's a bulletin board just listing job descriptions, usually dull ones, often out-of-date. Sometimes it's a maze of job-application software.

That's no way to make a good impression. Remember that even when candidates are just cruising your careers area out of curiosity, they are forming an impression of the company. (And, for that matter, they are forming an impression of the importance of talent to the company. If the careers area is a poor cousin to the slick home page or products list, what does that say?)

Your employer brand takes center stage on the home page of your careers site. Lead with your unique attributes—what makes you different from other employers? Showcase the tangible and intangible benefits of working in your shop. Say why you're a great employer. Better yet, have your employees say why you're great. Tell a first-time visitor what it takes to succeed at your shop.

Think about customer service. Fortune 1000 companies have help desks and customer service departments around the world. Even small businesses have help on their Web sites and an 800 number you can call. If you have any little problem, they help. Can't figure out how to get the toothpaste out of a tube of Crest? Procter & Gamble puts a toll-free number right on the tube. How often does the careers section of a Web site invite candidates to call a qualified recruiting specialist to help them apply for a job?

Even if you don't want to provide that degree of care, there are simple ways to make your recruiting site attract the best. Lori Erickson, Monster's senior vice president of global human resources, describes the basics:

> Having a great brand is necessary but not sufficient to bring great employees automatically to your company. Monster was built on a great brand—our commercials, our mascot, our advertising—but three years ago you could go on our own recruitment Web site, and you couldn't find out a lot about what working for Monster was like. All you could find was job postings and résumés. We were asking the product brand to bring candidates in the door.
>
> The careers section of your Web site needs to differentiate you in an authentic way from other employers who are competing for the talent you want. What will make an impact? People want the basic information, and they also want to envision what it would be like to work for your company. You should have pictures that promote the message you want to send.
>
> For example, Monster is located in a beautiful refurbished mill in Massachusetts. We have a big open area called the Monster Den, with murals of our mascot monsters, pool, and Ping-Pong and foosball tables, and big

overstuffed chairs. There's a gym and a store and great views. Our physical work environment is a selling feature, so we show it off on the recruiting site.

Forward-looking companies now include streaming video of the work environment, especially if they're trying to attract younger workers. Our videos feature employees at all levels and all positions. Diversity matters to us, so we try to weave that into the images of the company so that diverse candidates coming to check us out can feel, "Wow, I could be a contributor at this company."

Our culture is one of the biggest draws to the company, and attraction to our culture is an indicator of success, so we emphasize that in our recruitment Web site.

Big and small organizations are improving their careers area all the time. Even without technological bells and whistles, here are some baseline requirements you'll need in order to play:

- Have management and employees describe company goals, mission, culture, and values in a direct and informal way.
- Have your employees speak to the prospect—in Web pages or, better, with video testimonials.
- Make it easy to find the right job.
- Make it easy to apply for a job.
- Make it easy for those who don't find a job match to submit a résumé and cover letter anyway.
- Give confirming feedback when someone applies or writes.

If these requirements were easy to achieve, Web site designers would settle on a single solution and we could all go home. They are not easy, but fortunately a good basic candidate experience is neither difficult nor expensive to achieve. For example, the manager who assembles a job description can add a personal note about the significance of the job (anonymously, if you wish) like this one:

The best part of being a marketing assistant:

"Our customers come from all over the world. Anybody who is curious about people, who loves to persuade and loves to communicate will find that the job of marketing assistant is a graduate course in human nature."

—Jesse Harriott, VP, Global Monster Insights

Job Description Versus Job Advertisement

A good job description emphasizes what an employee has to achieve on a day-to-day basis and how success will be measured. A good job advertisement emphasizes why a qualified individual should apply for the job.

Notice we said *apply for the job*. That could mean finding out more information, filling out an online application, sending in a résumé, or picking up the phone. The key is that the candidate takes action.

The advertisement will list a job description's requirements, tasks, skills, and the like, but most ads stop there or they tack on a bit of boilerplate about the company. Good ads inspire the right people to throw their hats into the ring by weaving the employer brand message throughout the necessary information.

For example, if a central message is that you want people who can make decisions and act rather than deliberate, you'll emphasize that with phrases like "takes action quickly to satisfy customer needs," "XYZ Co. wants sales professionals who can act decisively," or "bring firm direction to department."

The following is a basic template for such an advertisement.

Ad Title

Not the job title, but an eye-catching title for the ad itself. Imagine a candidate wading through 23 ads titled "Legal Assistant" and then encountering the title "Need Legal Eagle with an Eagle Eye" or "Help Kids in Trouble with the Law." Candidates scan job ads like you scan résumés, so give them a reason to be interested!

Snapshot of The Job (What the Recruiter Is Looking For)

Start with a job title and quickly state the results you expect: "increase sales at least 20 percent," "delight patients with unexpected service," or "turn 50 percent of new customers into repeat customers."

Employer Brand Statement 1 (Including Intangible Benefits)

The next statement leads with intangible benefits of the job, based on your thinking about your employer brand, and tells the candidates what is uniquely in it for them. This can be specific to the job, as in "this superb team needs an innovative leader" (innovation and leadership are key), or to the company, as in "after 40 years without a layoff, XYZ Co. feels like a second family. We care about each other and our communities."

Why This Job Is Important

Again, refer to the heart of your employer brand. For example, if "pride" is a key message, tell why this particular job inspires pride: "the home service technicians are the face of XYZ Co. to our customers, and their pride in a job well done is key to our success." A direct statement from the manager here is particularly effective: "the manager of this position is looking for people who take pride in their work, their company, and themselves."

Basic Job Information

Responsibilities, tasks, required skills, and experience—all come from the job description. Ask yourself, "What's really required for the job?" This still allows you to filter responses according to your choice, but it doesn't take good candidates out of the running. If a quality is preferred but not required, say so.

Tangible Job Benefits (Salary, Benefits, Etc.)

Statements like "we offer competitive salary and benefits" are boilerplate, and candidates expect them. Unique tangible benefits can liven this up a bit; for example, if you have a membership deal with the local gym or day care center, say so.

Employer Brand Statement 2

Reinforce the heart of your employer brand. If candidates have read this far, they are interested. Now raise the emotional stakes by telling the skilled candidates why you really, truly believe this is the best organization they will find. Think about the poised candidates, who are now judging their current reality with a fantasy of working with you. Before you call them to action, talk about a benefit you offer that they should leave their current jobs to have. For example: "just as we believe in constant improvement in our products, we insist on constant growth for our people, and so we offer every employee tuition reimbursement, adult education classes, and on-site management training."

You can also reinforce the first employer brand statement. For example: "innovation is more than a slogan; it's a way of life for us; every year our employee product council awards more than $20,000 in special bonuses to fellow employees who have come up with innovative ideas."

Call to Action

If you want their résumés, "Apply Now!" is an okay statement. If you're really treating applicants like customers, think about them being online, reading your ad, two clicks away from your competitors' job listings. What can you promise (and deliver) that's different? An instant reply and a response within a week— either "No, thanks" for unqualified applicants or a phone call to good prospects? How about a response within three days? Is that promising a lot? Yes. Does it make you different? Yes!

There are two other calls to action that have become standard online: "e-mail this job to a friend," and "find out more about XYZ Co." If candidates choose either, you can use them to reinforce your interest. If they e-mail the job to a friend, have your system set up to send them a separate e-mail—thanking them and inviting them to send in a résumé to your database. If they click on a link to "find out more," direct them to a section of your organization's careers Web site, thanking them for their interest in careers at your company.

If you send them to the corporate home page you won't control the employment-branding message. You want to capture their interest in working for your company before sending them on to study the nice shiny products on the rest of your site.

That's not to say you can't use the product brands to advantage. McDonald's arranged to give away electronic coupons for McDonald's menu items to any-one who applied for a job from the Web site. Whether or not the person got a job, the company wanted to thank people for their interest. It leveraged all that consumer advertising money, and customer loyalty, to burnish its recruiting. Now, that's memorable.

Channels

You have a message. You know who should hear it. Now it's time to decide how to reach them—your communication channels.

We don't have to burden this discussion with a lot of marketing terms, but *channels* is a good one to define carefully. They are commonly thought of as con-duits that direct your messages, like water rushing through a channel. That's been true with mass media like television, radio, and newspapers. Because advertising in mass media is expensive and reaches a broad audience, recruiters have devised messages that appeal to the largest number of potential candidates.

The Internet permanently changed the landscape of channel advertising. Now channels are distinct and numerous, and the same media that reach millions can also target a very specific audience. The Internet is multidirectional in that it allows a message's recipient to reply or send the message to others, and it delivers a more customized response to that reply. This can continue right down to the ultimate employment marketing channel—one employer and one candidate finding each other. An employer can re-create this one-to-one channel for each candidate.

One example of multidirectional communication is the online job search agent. A poised candidate (employed or not) gives a Web site information on what he wants in a job. This information becomes a software "agent" that sends an e-mail alert whenever a job opening that fits the candidate's description appears. He then has the option to look into the job (and apply) or not. If the job openings in the e-mail are not a good match, the candidate can refine the search agent with more exact information. This set of interactions is a channel for the employer, and it gets better as the candidate refines his search agent.

Sometimes employers lose sight of the fact that Monster and other online career services are media vehicles that can expose their organization and job postings to over 20 million people a month. Unfortunately, employers don't treat their online media messages with the same level of scrutiny and branding as if they were trying to persuade an individual. Furthermore, recruiters forget that candidates treat online media in the same way that consumers treat products, and they are conditioned to search for relevance quickly; if they don't find it, they move on.

Recruiters work with job descriptions all day, so it's easy to forget that the typical job description is a densely composed list of tasks and requirements but offers little information about what it will feel like to work in a job. Will the work be satisfying? Interesting? Challenging?

Unlike print media (newspapers and magazines mostly, but also outdoor advertising and even window signs), a small business job advertisement can compete online with on a job ad from General Electric. Years ago a city's big businesses dominated the help wanted sections, and candidates browsed 80 pages of full-page and half-page advertisements before they got to the small guys. Now, Mary's Main Street Corner Pharmacy can compete with CVS for talent. The individual might care more that Mary's is 20 minutes closer to home than CVS. Some people want to work in a small business, where they know all the other employees, and smaller businesses try to link up with that segment of the poised workforce. That was much harder when the big guys buried their advertising; it's easy now.

This is how the candidate empowerment we discussed in Chapter 1 benefits employers who establish a very clear brand, because the level playing field means they can compete in new media. This is another reason that employer branding and strong, specific advertising is even more important on the Internet: armed with these, David can beat Goliath to the candidates who are looking for exactly what a smaller business can offer.

New media also poses new challenges: for recruiters, the hydra-headed problem of "overconnectedness" means a job advertisement can be seen by anyone, anywhere. There is a much greater burden on recruiters to encourage unqualified candidates not to apply. Rob O'Keefe of TMP Worldwide Advertising and Communications observes that overconnectedness has become a burden to the most talented candidates as well, because those recruiters who think they have too many applicants set up barriers to entry that can prevent the right people from applying for a position.

While Web sites function as media vehicles, they increasingly function also as meeting places, fueling the recent rise of social networking. (Even blogs link to other blogs. Many have "talk back" functions as well, so a number of voices appear in one place.) Shortly after a new service like MySpace, Facebook, or YouTube enters the popular imagination, employers are using it to recruit talent. (They also use dedicated networking sites and directories—thus, the current popularity of LinkedIn, Orkut, Ryze, ZoomInfo and others.) The ones who succeed are willing to embrace each particular service's audience, because communities have always coalesced around shared interests, methods, and values. Social networking sites will play an increasingly significant role in recruiting as particular audiences find their favorites.

How will we behave online in 5 or 10 years? Internet trends are notoriously difficult to predict accurately, and often one trend will influence another. For example, five years ago, Monster tested the concept of candidates getting alerted to new job openings by cell phone, but in America, the computer was so well entrenched that few candidates saw the need. Cell phone ownership in China, however, has so far outstripped computer ownership that the cell phone might become a significant medium for linking people up with jobs. In the same period, the handheld computer merged with the cell phone in the West. It could happen that these changes in technology and media will make the phone/handheld a significant job application platform.

This is more certain: when employers contact candidates, the message is more important, and more permanent, than the medium that delivers it. Individuals choose jobs for a mosaic of individual reasons; employers need to reach them with a message designed to appeal to the best profiled, best understood, and potentially highest achieving candidate.

This leaves recruiters with a neverending task of choosing the right channels, and they arrive at wise choices only after they have a deep understanding of the audience they want to reach, the message they have to send, and the channels available to them. After that, the choices are tactical, driven by results and return on investment.[1]

Sometimes print is appropriate, sometimes it's niche Web sites, sometimes it's large Internet career services, sometimes face-to-face methods like job fairs or campus recruiting. Given the number of Internet recruiting channels, the mobility and changing profiles of candidates, and the pace of technology, we think employers should review their outreach channels at least once a year.

Résumés Online

The Web is the ultimate channel for candidates to make themselves available to employers, in the form of résumé databases and personal Web sites. When employers or recruiters look for talent, they can locate it among the millions of résumés online or among the résumés stored in their individual corporate databases.

Whether the databases contain 2,000 or 20,000 or 20 million résumés, however, you need search tools and techniques that are powerful enough to find the right needle in that haystack. It's the same on the open Web: if you use a search term like *Harvard* you might end up with résumés containing Harvard Business School, Harvard Common Press, Harvard Pilgrim Health Plan, or Harvard, Illinois. Search tools are getting better all the time, so get educated in searching techniques and be thoughtful about how you search, whether it's in an online database, a corporate database, or out on the Web. (Searching is an entire discipline in itself, and there are people doing amazing work moving the field forward, both in tools and techniques.)

The poised job seekers who don't see your job posting (because they aren't checking job postings that week) probably have résumés posted online. They might still be open to your inquiry and will decide whether to respond based on the power of your brand and the relevance of the opportunity. Poised employees self-select those jobs or inquiries that they feel are important to them, which is why, even in a direct inquiry, your brand message has to be crystal clear.

When approaching these workers—those who are already employed but have put their résumés online, indicating they're poised—you also need to bear a realistic expectation of the response rate. When you reach out to people, a dozen personal or professional commitments might prevent them from applying for a job with you. Even then, however, your outreach is a branding opportunity, and your approach might set a job switch in motion six months from now.

With résumés online it's the same story as with reaching out through advertising: If you put all your energy into transactional hiring you're acting like a hunter, and you have to go out every day to find prey. If you put some energy into building relationships with poised candidates you're acting like a farmer, patiently working in anticipation of a big harvest later.

Even from a transactional point of view, résumé databases are a primary source of talent, and in a time of shortage you can't afford to ignore any source. You have a job to fill: you advertise broadly, you advertise in niches, you search your own database and other databases, and you search the Web. You search news sources and blogs and show up at professional meetings. You do what it takes to reach out and put your brand in the minds of the people you have to hire.

Public Presence

Publicity, public relations, "thought leadership," presence in media, and the public marketplace—the recruiters we admire use these strategic branding components with their eye on long-term goals. Look at a really powerful national or local employment brand, and you'll find people focused on its public presence.

Earlier, we suggested that you enlist the marketing department to help craft the final form of employer brand statements and job ads. Public presence is another activity in which you want to use a marketer's expertise. If you're in a company with 20 people and no marketing group, get help.

Caroline Brown, the senior manager of employment marketing at Home Depot, uses the company's product marketing prowess to reach potential employees. For example: "When we sponsored NASCAR, we put a quick recruitment message at the bottom of the NASCAR schedule cards that Home Depot sponsored." She adds, "With over 2,000 stores across the country, it's highly likely that most of our candidates are also our shoppers, and we know many of them are NASCAR fans." What better place to look for good employ ees than among your customers? Marketing knows where to find them.

Communicating your employer brand through commercial channels offers the benefit of bringing you closer in touch with the marketplace at large. Good public presence also starts a virtuous cycle around all hiring practices. We've talked about the need to keep your employer brand authentic, and your public statements are heard (and believed or disbelieved) by your own employees, who can tell you if the outside story matches the inside reality. Executives can support the effort, either internally or as public spokespersons.

Just as your employer brand needs to jive with your overall brand, your public presence as an employer needs to fit with broad publicity efforts, so get the perspective of your public relations person as you design outreach. Remind him that recruiting well benefits the public relations effort (another virtuous cycle, if it's done right).

Public presence, large and small, can consist of multiple and simultaneous efforts, such as

- **Traditional publicity and public relations.** Press releases and interviews with local and national business press can tell the world what it's like to work for you. Public relations work can broadcast your employees' involvement in company-sponsored charity work; this attracts people who share the same commitment.
- **Internal publicity.** Any organization with more than 10 members seems prone to compartmentalization. If you want people to support better hiring, you have to talk up your efforts, explain the value of your work, and promote the integrated discipline we've discussed. Leaders must understand the value of this approach in terms of profit and/or achieving the organization's mission. With Internal newsletters, Intranets, company meetings, employee referral programs, and the like, make sure that everyone knows what you're doing in every possible way. This doesn't just apply to professional recruiters or HR staff; hiring managers who know the value of talent have to spread the word internally.
- **Employee voices.** Employee testimony on your Web site is positive; employee testimony off your site is persuasive. Get your best people out there on their own blogs, and don't censor what they say. Send them to conferences and recruiting events. Give them time to network, even when it's not part of your referral program. Pay for a big party at your workplace—the only price of admission is that employees bring a friend. Train ambassadors to work the floor and talk up your organization. (Remember branding's "Reasons to Believe" attribute? Unfiltered raves saying, "This is a great place to work" are priceless.)
- **Professional presence.** Your employees at every level should be present in the professional associations, clubs, and gatherings in your field.

Managers can serve, teach, and network within both their industry and their discipline; for example, a financial manager of a reprographics firm might be active in both the state accounting board and the International Reprographic Association. Active membership is both good for professional exposure and networking to locate talent.

- **Presence on campus.** College recruiting is familiar for businesses seeking both new graduates and advanced graduates; every fall recruiters fan out to business and law schools, and every spring they go to likely undergraduate campuses. The best recruiting groups seek niches on other campuses. For example, Valero Energy keeps close relationships with technical schools and community colleges as it looks for skilled workers to run its refineries and pipelines. Hospitals and nursing homes sponsor programs for nursing aides and assistants as early as high school.

- **Thought leadership.** Thought leadership means people in your company advance the field with innovations in business methods, product development, data, or technology. Watching the employment landscape, poised candidates notice which firm is leading their field intellectually. Who is pushing the industry forward? Where will they learn the most? Who employs people they want as managers, mentors, and models of innovation?

  Thought leadership is typically showcased by publishing and presenting research and white papers, by presenting seminars live and online ("webinars"), by acquiring patents, by taking a stand on public issues of concern to the industry, and by taking a leading role in an industry's changing profile. Thought leadership attracts attention, publicity, interest, and good candidates.

  One caution: don't try to fake thought leadership. It requires original and sustained contributions, not me-too press releases or halfhearted "findings."

- **Awards.** Being named a "Best Place to Work," whether by *Fortune* magazine or your local business journal, isn't just an honor—it should become part of your public presence at every opportunity. The same goes for distinctions like "Most Admired" or "Employer of Choice" praise from any media. They're the first answer to the in-demand candidate's question,

"Why should I work for you?" You can become more visible to the people who award these distinctions, but the only way to win them is to create a great workplace.

Any legitimate award of this kind is a fringe benefit of a great work culture, not its goal, but if you have such a culture, promote it. Talk to local
media (and/or awarding organizations). Tell them why your organization
is a great employer. Study previous award winners for ways in which you
can improve. If you're too small to come to the notice of *Fortune* magazine,
remember that its list consists of a tiny fraction of businesses, and the more
effective distinction might come from your professional association or city
magazine. If legitimate bloggers praise you, let people know it on your Web
site. These are all reasons to believe in your employment brand.

Being a best place to work takes more than providing free donuts and
a foosball table; it's creating a culture that has employees actively telling
others to join them in your tremendous enterprise. And to quote an old
song, that takes personality.

Personality

If you're going to brag, have something to brag about. Recruiter Kelly Hogan
describes the work culture at Eze Castle Software; notice how her "sell" is simply constructed on the details of their distinct culture—so distinct we'd call it
a personality:

> Monday through Thursday are business-casual days. Friday is just casual.
> Wednesday and Friday we get together to mingle, so you can talk to indi-
> viduals that you don't interact with all the time. You will see the CEO there;
> you'll see the president, the VPs, and the managers there, chatting with
> other employees.
>
> We provide yearlong training and certification. We have a mentor pro-
> gram and want you to use it. We celebrate our global cultures on
> International Potluck day, when people from around the world bring in

their favorite food. You might work with executives on the Improvement Committee, which thinks about how we can work better together, or the Community Service Committee.

Another thing that we like to do is called the Chore Wheel. Instead of hiring outside services to come stock our chips and coffee, everybody pitches in. So you might team up six times a year with the president or your boss or another executive to empty the dishwasher or stock the chips, deliver the mail, or put out the fruit in bowls around the office.

Nobody is exempt from these chores. It's part of a pitch-in mentality that's also how we work together. We want you to feel like this is your home away from home, because there are times where you're going to be putting in long hours, and you are going to need to just stay here longer. And you might as well enjoy the workspace that you're in. We're all in this together.

Kelly's described a lot of perks, but underlying all these goodies is a shared sense of responsibility, excitement, and growth. A CEO doesn't have to deliver mail, and it might not be the most efficient use of his or her time—but what's the value to a talented new recruit of seeing the big boss pitching in? In Eze Castle Software's particular culture, it's priceless. That recruit will talk to friends about this amazing employer. Personality encourages those referrals, and word of mouth has always been the most powerful way of getting the message out.

Employee Referral Programs

In the last few years, employee referral programs grew to be regarded as hiring's "killer application." Everybody said they wanted 30 percent, 50 percent, or more of their new hiring to come from employee referrals. Like most killer apps, however, referral programs must be intimately connected to a bigger picture. They also require a lot of care and feeding to get right.

When it comes to referral programs, our research finds a disconnect between manager and employee perceptions. While 81 percent of employers believe employee word of mouth strongly influences candidate opinion, only

33 percent of employers involve their employees in promoting the employer brand. While 66 percent of employers believe they effectively communicate key employer branding elements, only 30 percent of employees say their organization promotes the benefits of working there. If employees don't know the message, how can they be ambassadors for the brand?[2] Something's broken here; so let's review how a good referral program connects to the rest of recruiting.

Employee referral programs reward current employees for bringing candidates into the company. A typical program pays employees a bonus after people they have referred land a job at the company.

The logic of using employees to bring in candidates is strong:

- Employees know what it takes to succeed at a company, and they understand its culture, so they tend to refer appropriate candidates.
- Employees know others with similar skills, such as former coworkers, schoolmates, members of networking groups, and friends.
- Employees have seen others (typically former coworkers) under actual workplace conditions, not just in the context of a job interview.
- Employees in a referral program have a double interest in locating strong candidates—to earn a referral bonus in the short term and increase the long-term success of the company.
- Employees know individuals who are not actively looking for a job but are poised to move.
- Employees who are careful of their reputations recommend only highly skilled candidates.
- Employee referral programs can be less expensive over time than other methods.

Employee referral programs also have pitfalls:

- People tend to know people like themselves, and most referral programs do little to encourage diversity in the workplace (either social/demographic diversity or a diversity of talent).

- People's closest circles of acquaintance tend to be within a small geographic area, and this limits the pool of potential hires who might relocate.

- Amateur recruiters are much less experienced than managers or professional recruiters at judging whether a candidate has the right level of skills for the job. The referral system is a pipeline for finding candidates, not for making final decisions.

- Careful record keeping and rules are needed to ensure, for example, that two employees don't both claim to have made a referral. (Does the first to refer get the reward? What happens if employee A makes a referral that doesn't result in a hire, and a year later employee B refers the same person, who then does get hired?)

- If it's too complicated, people won't play.

- Employees need to be trained to use the system effectively.

- In larger organizations, referral programs need to be publicized steadily to remain active. Otherwise they become part of the amorphous grab bag of benefits used by just a few employees. (Also, when someone refers a friend, he expects that friend to get red-carpet treatment, or at least a quick phone call. It's a good expectation, so follow up quickly on referrals.)

- The programs cost money and time to run. Cost-effectiveness needs to be calculated against other methods.

> *Employees know what it takes to succeed at their company, and they understand its culture, so they tend to refer appropriate candidates.*

At their best, employee referral programs become part of an organization's culture, even integral to the employer brand if you use words like *teamwork* or *reward for initiative*. To achieve their potential, they need active understanding, support, and promotion from top to bottom. If the lowliest junior assistant brings in five good employees because he's well networked and active, the CEO should stand him up in front of the entire company and cheer (better yet, he should hand the guy a check in front of everyone).

The more people who participate, the larger your potential pool for referrals. Why stop at your employees? How about extending your referral program to contractors, vendors, and customers? How about former employees? If you run a pet store, take down that "Help Wanted" sign and put up a poster saying "Send us a great employee and get a month of food for your pet!" Run a physical therapy practice? How about offering every customer who brings you a successful hire five free visits?

There's room for experimentation here. Referral programs work best when people have a personal stake in referring only the best candidates (not just friends). Some programs exempt managers over a certain pay grade, because it's part of their job to be on the lookout for talent. If you really want to cast the net of your referral program wide, the only people you should clearly exempt from a reward system are those who are already paid to find people—for example, recruiters. (If the executives don't want to collect a reward, donate it to a local charity and publicize it.) Several online businesses are trying to bring the referral-for-pay concept to the Web at large, offering clients proprietary networks of people who make good referrals.

Are you ready for an employee referral system to succeed? To paraphrase Professor Frederick Reichheld (from his excellent book *The Ultimate Question*), what really matters is whether your current employees would recommend your organization to their friends.

Chris Forman, president of human resources consulting firm AIRS, believes that you train amateur recruiters by telling stories. He says: "Employees remember stories. Right now we're looking for customer service representatives, so I told people, 'I was out to dinner the other night and I had the best waitress in the world. She was phenomenal. She was smart, she was there, she was on time, and I gave her a 30 percent tip. And at the end I gave her my business card and said, you know what, if you ever get sick of this, give us a holler.' People get that. I tell our engineers that when they attend a meeting of the Upper Valley [Connecticut River] Engineers Club, they should go up to the smartest person in the room and say, 'You're the smartest person in the room. I would really love to have you work with me. Why? Because you're the smartest person in the room.' "

Chris points out that a good referral system can break old rules, for example, about hiring relatives. "This might sound counterintuitive, but we love nepotism. We have brothers-in-law and sisters who work here. My father works in the business. They're our best employees. You never hire two people at once, but when people say don't hire friends, neighbors, or relatives, they might be overlooking great candidates."

There are plenty of ways to set up an employee referral program, from the most informal bonus system in a small organization to a full-blown system that identifies and tracks the employees who make the greatest contribution. Managers can offer additional incentives to people who bring new hires into their departments. Individuals might receive a better raise based on the performance of the people they bring in. You can teach essential networking skills to every employee and broadcast victory stories. You can offer a portion of the reward when a referral is hired and the rest after 3, 6, or 12 months.

Rob O'Keefe of TMP Worldwide Advertising and Communications suggests a variation he calls a "preferral" program:

A referral program works on the premise that an employer notifies employees about open positions and employees think about who they know that would meet the requirements and do well in the organization, and then rise to action.

A preferral program first focuses on identifying employer brand evangelists at the height of their evangelism (when they first join the company), and staying with them throughout their employment experience. It asks these evangelists to identify potential referrals across all positions in the organization, regardless of whether they are open or not.

In other words, use employees to fill the pipeline with candidates before you need them. Intelligent engagement by employees who promote your employer brand is the ultimate outreach. It belongs in any recruiting program, in any recruiting discipline. Its common name is networking.

The Professional Network

Anyone who hires needs a network. We can't say it more simply than that.

Pick your metaphor: a pipeline of steadily arriving candidates, a pool of talent from which to draw, or a stack of résumés in a database. However you picture it, an active talent network is the way to get off the linear track of transactional, time-pressed, emergency hiring. A recruiter's network of poised workers, from long-term prospects to company alumni, gets the virtuous Engagement Cycle of Attract, Acquire, and Advance moving, and keeps that cycle turning.

We hardly have to convince full-time recruiters of the importance of networking or teaching the basics. But for the hiring manager who relies too heavily on the HR department, for the entrepreneur or small business owner, networking needs to be demystified.

Hiring comes down to the relationship between a single candidate and a single employer, whether that employer is a professional recruiter, manager, business owner, or HR generalist. We've talked about getting the message out because in a world of mobile talent, you have to be known to many in order to connect with the right few candidates. At some point, that outreach results in the "in-reach" of a candidate agreeing to have some kind of professional relationship, and that is the beginning of a network.

A professional network is not a passive list of names but a never-ending set of active relationships. You might have heard this before, but let it sink in for a moment. Are you really maintaining a large set of relationships with potential candidates? Relationships confirmed not just in a single e-mail but also over weeks, months, and years of interaction?

MY POV

"I was talking to a senior VP of HR not too long ago, and he said to me, 'You know, I wonder why recruiters never call trying to entice me to their organizations. They always just call me and ask me who I know.'

"I said, 'You don't get it! All those recruiters are hoping you would say, 'Yeah, this job sounds good to me.' " Most of the time those conversations begin with a request for a referral, with the hope that the person on the other end would realize, Wow, this job sounds like something I would want to do."

–John Wilson, Wilson Recruiting

There are a hundred excuses for neglecting a network. You have demands and deadlines at work. Networking doesn't promise a quick payoff. There are a lot of dead ends. You're not the type to shake hands at a networking event. You're just not the networking type. You own the cable franchise and the service technician just quit, and the customers are calling; you can't run off to a networking meeting and build a lot of long-term relationships with potential cable service technicians . . . you need to fill the job *now*.

Nevertheless, a large and active network of poised workers is the best source of good hires. It's worth the investment of time to add it to your portfolio. (Note: Executive search consultants, working at the highest levels of recruiting, consistently rely on long-term relationships to fill those top positions. You can do the same for positions at any level; all that changes is the places you'll find potential candidates.)

Assuming you do want to build a professional network of potential candidates, you can start with these simple habits, which we see in every good networking recruiter's behavior.

Start with Trusted Relationships

Trust is the glue that holds together a good network, so start with the people you already know. Enlist colleagues, friends, past and present employees, and existing candidates in your networking. If you interviewed impressive candidates in the last two years but didn't hire them, get back in touch. Ask everyone with whom you have a conversation about work, "Whom do you know?"

Get into Groups

All professional associations have at least two purposes, and the second is networking. If you want to hire Web designers who know how to make easy-to-use Web sites, you can attend the meetings of associations of Web designers, usability specialists, advertising, or large computer/multimedia interests.

Go Where the Résumés Are Located

Dip into your company résumé database or the file you keep labeled "people to watch." Access online résumé databases and learn to search for résumés online. Look for connections: Who went to school with you? Who worked in companies next to you? Who works for your competitors, or your suppliers, or in a related field? Who satisfies these criteria *and* lives within a 20-mile radius? Think creatively about résumés you've viewed in the past. Who was promising but not experienced? Who was looking for the wrong job? Who moved away (but might have moved back)?

It's easy to find résumés—it takes more work to cultivate relationships once you locate people. But it works. Online you can find someone you worked closely with three jobs and many years ago. (Try it—search the Web with the name of a company you worked for, and some names. You'll find old colleagues.)

MY POV

"There are really two kinds of recruiting, that I call virtual and relationship recruiting. Virtual recruiting is about the here and now. It's about having a requisition for a SQL server database administrator in Arizona and putting that together with a candidate you just found in Boston, with the most competitive offer humanly possible. Relationship recruiting is about the long-term conversation you develop with the candidate—what their lifetime objectives are, whether they have kids, where do they live, what's important to them, how they make decisions. But more importantly, it's not about the job you're ready to deliver today; it's about coming together two jobs from now."

—*Jeff Gore, Stride & Associates*

Go Where the Candidates Go

You might be wary of attending meetings of job seeker groups, thinking you'll be deluged with inappropriate résumés, and in fact it sometimes happens. But what about the people who work with candidates in transition? Campus career centers, career coaches, and outplacement professionals all connect to potential talent and don't rely on you for their pay. Even people who run informal job seeker support groups—the kind that gather once a week in church meeting rooms—can be sophisticated networkers.

Network Online (but Use Your Head)

Participation in online networking can help feed your pipeline. These sites aren't yet a substitute for face-to-face or phone networking conversations. There's an intimacy to the latter that's lost when connecting through strangers. Social networking sites and interest groups (such as association Web sites) can supply connections, once you're practiced in using them while not becoming a target of unqualified candidate inquiries.

Take an Interest in More Than the Job

Networking means listening. Ask about people's experiences, values, and ambitions. Find out what they like about their current jobs and what could be better. Get the subjective story that's hard to know from a résumé, and which someone might not tell you in a more circumspect moment (like when they're applying for a job).

Be Helpful

Every great networker we know offers help to people without asking for a reward. Call it good manners, good business (because people want to pay you back), or just good karma, but time and again those who ask "what can I do for you?" establish relationships that result in finding great candidates. The open-handed offer of help is an act of friendship that introduces trust to a network relationship.

Follow Up

Think about it: most recruiters, hiring managers, and HR people encounter so many people in the course of a week that they develop an "on-to-the-next-one" habit. In Chapter 6 we suggested you offer a newsletter to keep in touch with promising (but not-quite-ready) candidates. That's a passive communication. When you encounter people who are really of interest, or really connected to many potential candidates, put a big red FOLLOW UP sign on their business cards or tuck their résumés in a special file. Then call them every few months and talk—how's it going, who do you know, what can I do for you?

When you've established these habits, go ahead and work more formally on networking to recruit. There are professional networking seminars, courses from resources like the Society for Human Resource Management (SHRM) or Business Network International (BNI), and good books (you'll find a couple in the Resources section beginning on page 215).

Watch executive recruiters in action and you'll quickly see that they believe in the open-hand method of managing relationships. That is, they establish long-term relationships with no guarantee of a direct payoff. This builds up trust in candidates who are more likely to listen to the recruiters later, when the time comes to fill a position.

Tactics for Acute Shortages

This entire book is about hiring during the talent shortages to come; some businesses, as we noted in Chapter 1, are already strained by a dearth of certain talents. The most acute examples we know are in health care. Nurses, pharmacists, radiologists, medical technicians . . . that's just the beginning. Joseph Cabral, vice president and chief human resources officer of North Shore-LIJ Health System, describes how shortages pervade the business today:

> As the health-care industry has evolved over the years, recruiting talent for difficult-to-fill positions has become even more challenging. Many of our positions require skills beyond a particular expertise, such as IT, for example, where a position may require both a technical and a clinical background. On the flip side, there's a misconception that we will only recruit candidates with a clinical background or prior experience in health care. The types of skills and backgrounds we seek are unique to the individual positions, and each situation may be different based upon the requirements.

Health-care organizations face expanding technology, expanding demand, a pressing financial situation, and radical change. For example, electronic medical records need to be unified to improve patient care and efficiency, but today they exist on many incompatible systems.

How are hospitals and others coping?

For one thing, they aren't relying on one source of candidates. Talk to a medical recruiter today and he'll tell you that he's using every available technique, from Internet advertising to definitive branding to overseas recruiting to holding networking groups and social events for nurses and others.

Lesson one for a shortage: diversify your portfolio of recruiting tools. Go through these chapters and use every technique we've described. Get the entire organization involved.

Lesson two: if you can't find talent, make talent. Increasingly, hospitals are supporting education, and establishing close relationships with educational institutions. In San Antonio, Barry Burns of Methodist Healthcare System instituted scholarships at a new pharmacy school. Recruiters are driving down past colleges and talking to high school students about medical careers and keeping in touch.

Lesson three: hold on to what you have. A shortage tends to up the recruiting budget but also threatens to burn out the workers whose skills are in short supply.

Lesson four: put at least as much energy into retention as you do into recruitment, and you'll spend less time replacing those who leave (see Chapter 9).

When the Word Works

The Attract stage of the Attract, Acquire, and Advance Engagement Cycle, at its best, is a long chain of experiences: talented candidates hear about you from an advertisement, a recommendation, or a referral; they decide to find out more, and ask around or check you out online; they approach you or you approach them. This experience is similar to the one consumers have with a brand and a product.

Phil Knight, the longtime head of Nike, told employees "we have nothing but our brand." Knight and Nike live that belief so thoroughly that many employees call themselves an "Ekin" (spell it backwards) and proudly sport a swoosh tattoo. The consistent brand message is sent through many channels for many reasons, and its most important quality is that it is compelling. The power of these consistent, compelling messages is the power to build an emotional intimacy with your target customer—the highly skilled candidate—one that will bring candidates to your door. And that's the beginning of the Acquire stage.

Review

- An employer brand message must be the theme of all outreach, starting with a candidate-centered recruitment Web site.
- Job advertisements are based on job descriptions but serve the particular imperatives of attracting the right people, and thus they must be distinct from descriptions.
- From advertising to résumé databases to social networking, channels must be understood as media consumers as potential carriers for your message.
- Referral and networking programs can be effective, but both must be designed to separate target candidates from message-carrying candidates.

Chapter 8

Bring in the Best

When Jim O'Mahony was the CEO of advertising agency Saatchi & Saatchi in Sydney, Australia, he knew that one hiring decision was so critical to success that he threw out the rulebook and created an extraordinary job interview. Jim tells the story:

The most important thing in our business is having the right CEO/creative director partnership. If you truly, truly have that right, everything works. The organization works well, new business comes through, the work is brilliant, the planning director's great, the finance director's happy—everything's wonderful.

I was looking for a new creative director for Sydney, and I found a candidate who was based in New York. Here was the job interview: We spent three days together in Los Angeles. We walked on the beach together, we ate together, we drank together, went to the movies together, went to stores together. We talked the whole time. We would go back and revisit subjects and develop ideas, just as if we were working together.

I could have given him every psychometric test under the sun . . . but spending three days together with him, talking about work, families, dreams, and aspirations—that's how I truly knew what he felt, who he was, how he would do his best work.

Was he a good hire? In May 2007 an industry organization voted him the number one executive creative director in Australasia, and his office the hottest agency in Australaisa. O'Mahony's unorthodox interview style—focused only on what was truly important—paid off beautifully.

What would persuade you to conduct a three-day job interview? In Jim's case, it was the prospect of creating the key relationship out of which every other success would emerge.

It's time to treat all candidates as if they were that important. Here, in the Acquire period of the Attract, Acquire, and Advance cycle, you are going to sort through all those people you attracted and all those poised workers you located. You're going to decide whom you want and how to land them.

We cannot overstate the impact of this phase on the people who will make or break your organization. While it is the shortest period of the three, typically lasting a few days or weeks, the dynamics between employer and candidate during the Acquire phase set the tone for the relationship that follows. Does your behavior, and the behavior of everyone a candidate meets during the interview process, validate or destroy the employer brand that drew that candidate in the first place? Are you building a back-and-forth business conversation, with both sides learning the critical information? Are you establishing trust, showing respect, and beginning the onboarding process before a candidate officially becomes an employee? If you are, then your Acquire process is working.

You can't spend three days with every prospect, but you can treat all prospects as if joining your team will be one of their most important decisions. Honor the significance of their interest, even as you make the decision whether or not to hire.

We've made the point that the poised, and talented, candidate is in control, and this really shakes up the Acquire phase. Managers tend to believe that once someone's a candidate, the hiring decision is fully up to the employer. In the world of the consumer candidate, however, the Acquire phase leads to two hiring decisions, one by the employer and one by the candidate.

Strong candidates learn to study the employer, the market, and themselves, and present a winning impression; a "sales pitch" carefully tailored to the job under discussion. This is the right way to make a good impression and land the job. Today, it behooves employers to study the candidate, the market, and themselves, and present a compelling impression from the moment a candidate comes to their attention to the time they join the organization—and beyond.

Jim O'Mahony sent a strong message to the candidate in Los Angeles: "you merit this kind of treatment." He learned a lot about his potential creative director in the three days they spent together, and he also invited the candidate to learn a lot about him, his organization, and the job. It was not a sure thing (Jim was asking a highly paid professional with a family to move 10,000 miles/16,000 kilometers to a new country). He was selling in the best way possible—by learning so much, and sharing so much, that the right decision would be made by both parties.

This chapter is about the practice that recruiting professionals call *selection*. Simply put, it means you have to choose among qualified candidates. Your judgment is based along two axes: what candidates *can do*, which you determine from their proven skills, experience, knowledge, education, and past behavior, and what they *will do*, based on their temperament, motivations, values and beliefs, and (again) past behavior.

The Funnel

The selection process looks like the classic sales funnel, by which a sales professional starts with a universe of prospects and works step by step to the "close." (We'll use the term *close* in this book to indicate the final agreement between candidate and employer.) It looks like Figure 8-1.

Figure 8-1

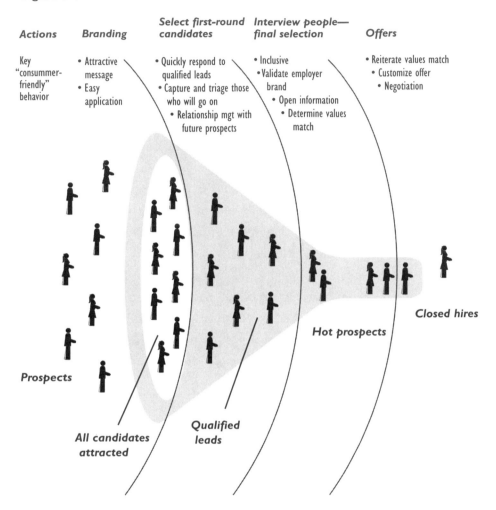

Actions	Branding	Select first-round candidates	Interview people— final selection	Offers
Key "consummer-friendly" behavior	• Attractive message • Easy application	• Quickly respond to qualified leads • Capture and triage those who will go on • Relationship mgt with future prospects	• Inclusive • Validate employer brand • Open information • Determine values match	• Reiterate values match • Customize offer • Negotiation

Prospects

All candidates attracted

Qualified leads

Hot prospects

Closed hires

A manager in a huge multinational enterprise and the line manager of a smaller business go through the same steps. The enterprise might make more use of technology, and probably has specialists (such as people whose only job is filling the funnel). At a smaller business, the line manager might be responsible for the entire process. These matters of scale don't much change the emotional experience of the candidates, however. They still find your organization (or are found by you), they still get interviewed, and they still check the validity of your employer brand. If your brand stresses efficiency and great business operations, for example, your method of moving candidates through the selection process had better be efficient or the people you want will doubt the brand.

However big your organization, or whatever business you're in, there are some simple steps you can take to foster a healthy and persuasive selection process.

Enlist Your Coworkers Early

You have already worked with the hiring manager and others to design job descriptions, advertisements, or postings. With candidates ready to interview, open the process to other departments with whom you work. Determine who should interview a candidate by examining the "ecosystem" of the job. Who depends on this job being done right (for example, others in the department, customers, and people next in the production chain)? Who is the right mentor for this person? Is there a technical skill that should be judged by an expert, whether that's computer programming or operating a forklift? Who might be a candidate's manager two years down the line?

Engaging others in your company is tantamount to planning the career trajectory of a great candidate at your organization. While predictions are subject to change, this kind of in-depth thinking takes you far beyond the checklist hiring that creates an average workforce. Get hiring managers and peers to talk about who is affected by the job, and how, and where someone might move— up, down, or sideways—and you're anticipating the inevitable, which is change.

At some point, distributing responsibility for hiring can become cumbersome. Google, once famous for a long and demanding interview process, recently streamlined its methods.[1]

The key players are those who ultimately have accountability for the position's expected results. Distribute information, distribute interviews, but limit the hiring decision to the people who will manage the employee.

Some smart recruiters bring in a "wild-card" interviewer specifically to answer any uncomfortable questions the candidate may have. This might be a peer who can describe working conditions in confidence. It might be a specialist who can answer the really hard questions that hiring managers might be reluctant to discuss ("What about that discrimination lawsuit last year?" "How do you feel about working for a company that sells cigarettes at its retail outlets?"). Just the presence of such a person demonstrates confidence and respect for the candidate.

Even in a small company, get several perspectives. If Mary down the hall has a track record of hiring good people, ask her to interview your candidate. That goes for the people who roll the trucks as well as the owner of the business. Do you think this is unrealistic? Who knows the customers better than the person who calls at their homes? If you believe that the manager is the only person equipped to evaluate a candidate, you could be cutting yourself off from critical information and cutting the candidate off from an opportunity to see how your employer brand is lived by your people.

Train the People Who Touch the Candidate

"I'll just talk to them and I'll know whether they'll work out."

"I just have to ask one question and then I'll give you a decision."

"I can look at their résumé and decide."

How many times have recruiting professionals heard these condescending (and frankly ignorant) sentiments? The track record of amateur interviewers speaks for itself—decisions made on the thinnest of presumptions or prejudices, followed by long regrets and recriminations.

If you're an HR or recruiting professional, get top management support for an interview-training program. Get a good interviewing book into the hands of managers.

If you're a manager (and especially if you've ever used expressions similar to those above), get training. Read about interviewing. Learn its pitfalls. For example, managers often forget that candidates feel exposed and a little vulnerable. When managers acknowledge that to the candidate, they show empathy, and the conversation goes better.

Get the Simple Stuff Right

When customers visit Monster's headquarters, we take them to the Monster Den, our big common room, before an appointment. We always ask, "Which of these eight kinds of coffee, tea, or water would you like? Do you want to relax until the appointment's ready?" We say, "Look around, get comfortable. Do you need a quiet place to write notes or make phone calls?" Customers feel welcome.

Candidates aren't treated any differently. In the Monster Den, we can always tell who the outsiders are, because they're the ones wearing suits. But you have to look carefully to know whether they're a candidate being interviewed for a job or a customer being interviewed about his or her business.

This effort does not cost a lot of money, and it separates us from our competitors for talent with surprising strength. Even unsuccessful candidates remember the Den and the way they were treated.

This is just one example of a simple step done right.

Do the Simple Stuff Fast

Make five simple improvements in the selection process in the next 30 days. Instigate an autoresponse and follow-up system for résumés you receive. Answer candidates' thank-you notes. Get a parking spot for candidates. Call managers on the morning of an interview and remind them to study the candidate's résumé. If you're a manager, block out 30 minutes before the interview to prepare. Automate these behaviors where possible, or make them habits.

Do the Hard Stuff Right, by Giving It the Time It Deserves

Learn to interview, learn to negotiate, and get help where you need it. If hiring were easy, we'd all have perfect organizations, contented workforces, and zooming profit margins.

Secret Shopper

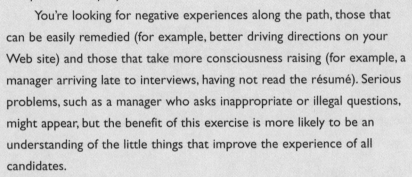

Retail stores employ secret shoppers to understand their customers' experience. You might do the same with your interview process, that is, send a bogus candidate through a set of interviews, then debrief him on the experience and identify ways to improve. You might do this with a trusted colleague from a non-competitive company.

You're looking for negative experiences along the path, those that can be easily remedied (for example, better driving directions on your Web site) and those that take more consciousness raising (for example, a manager arriving late to interviews, having not read the résumé). Serious problems, such as a manager who asks inappropriate or illegal questions, might appear, but the benefit of this exercise is more likely to be an understanding of the little things that improve the experience of all candidates.

A quicker version of this exercise is simply to walk through the interview process yourself, noting all the "touch points" a candidate experiences, from parking, to the reception area, to how many managers you meet and why. You'll find places to improve.

Finally, some HR managers we know have debriefed second-place or "silver-medal" candidates, encouraging them to keep a relationship with the organization, and soliciting advice on improving the interviewing experience. Just asking for their input shows respect (and they'll stay open to job offers in the future).

Market, Don't Sell

Peter Drucker's wisdom bears repeating here: the aim of marketing is to make selling superfluous. That means the funnel should identify the best candidates who are inclined to take the job and move them along, and take disinclined candidates graciously out of the process. All candidates have choices; by the time you get to the late interview stage, you should be talking to candidates who not only can do the job but are inclined to work with you because they share the organization's values, believe in its mission, and seem like a good fit with its managers and peers. To paraphrase Drucker: "the job fits her, and it sells itself."

How does this work? Assuming candidates are there because you identified them well and marketed the job to them through your employer brand, the later-stage interviews should be focused on increasingly intangible factors such as growth potential and organizational fit. In other words, the farther you get down the funnel, the more candidates are judged on unique matches with your organization. What makes them special is what makes you special.

Candor is one key: demonstrate the importance of the values decision upfront, by making it part of the early qualifying rounds (such as phone interviews). Wear your employment brand on your sleeve.

Be open about the criteria on which you will decide the best candidate.

Another key is to create a reliable feedback loop along the way. Review the candidates who have made the cut and those who have not. If the interview is a group effort, gather specific impressions of the candidate(s) along the way.

There are points in the process when you promote the job to candidates you want. Expert sales managers use a variety of techniques for this (with names like consultative selling, SPIN selling, and so on), and in the hiring process, this amounts to listening and understanding the candidate's individual situation. What about the job and your employer brand are really important to the candidates? Given that they can make the same money and benefits elsewhere, what internal rewards will attract them more to you?

Managers commonly forget the fact that every candidate is the center of her employment universe. It is irrelevant to the candidate if you have had to look at 100 résumés, give 10 phone interviews, and have three in-person interviews to reach this point in the process. It's equally irrelevant to you if the candidate has considered and rejected other employers before being attracted to your brand. You are addressing one person with a unique set of needs and a unique point of view. Your curiosity about the candidate's potential, needs, and desires allows you to relate those to the job position. The job becomes, in sales terms, a *solution* to the candidate's situation (wanting a better job).

Incidentally, selling doesn't mean painting a rosy picture of a job to land a hot candidate. Sandy Lewis, director of human resources at consulting company iP Capital Group, Inc., describes one way she knows her process is working: "We are brutally honest about the bad parts of the job as well as the good. That's part of selling the company, not the job. It's a compliment when an employee says, 'Sandy, this job is exactly what you and the others told me it was going to be.' It means we got the interview process right."

We'll say more about this later in this chapter, in the section titled "Closing the Candidate" on page 142.

Make the Hiring Authority Accountable for Results

Forcing strangers into a relationship causes disaster in blind dates, nation building, and business. If a manager is responsible for someone's performance, she has to have a say in the hiring. You can think of situations where this isn't possible—a new manager coming in, for example—but strive to connect accountability and responsibility for the hire.

MY POV

"We engage the manager all along because the candidate is forming the relationship with her, not Susie Smith in the HR Department. At the end of the day, people don't stay because the HR team guys did a great job bringing them in. They stay because of their manager, the leader, and their opportunity for growth."

—*Trish Backer-Miceli, Vice President of Human Resources, MedStar, Inc.*

Keep Track of How You Are Doing

If you understand how past behavior created current results, you can correct mistakes and repeat victories. This means identifying who made the best hiring decisions, and how they did it. What do they ask in interviews? Are their job advertisements or job descriptions superior?

You learn these details by following the path of candidates through the funnel. Ask these questions:

- Where did our best candidates come from (word of mouth, employee referrals, résumé databases, our Web site, or other sources)?
- Did we reach out to find them, or did they approach us?
- How quickly did we start a dialogue with prospects?
- How many prospects came from résumés we had on file or in our database?
- Did the candidates know where they were in the process (or did they fall into the "black hole")?
- How many good hires were made internally (for example, moving from one department to another)?
- Did the cost of finding the best candidate differ from other hiring? Why or why not?
- How long did the hiring process take from beginning to end?

Large enterprises, with dedicated recruiting staff, have the wherewithal to perform a more-detailed analysis, comparing their performance against benchmarks such as those established by HR consulting company Staffing.org, a provider of recruiting performance metrics. You can discover who hires best by looking at relative performance of employees in their first months.

Put all these data in the hopper and you might find some surprises. For example, one source of hiring or one manager might produce top performers that don't stay for long and have to be replaced. Whether that hiring pattern is cost-effective depends on how much profit they produce versus the aggregate cost of more frequent hiring (starting over every two years is costly—see "The Cost of Turnover" in Chapter 9).

If you orient your treatment of the consumer-minded candidate around the promises of your employment brand, every stage along the funnel that is your selection process will serve a double purpose: you will sharpen your organization's practice of selecting candidates, and you will help maintain a larger set of talented candidates who might one day join your organization as well as act as positive promoters of your brand. Although you can hire only a few, you can project your brand message to all and thus strengthen your hand in the quest for quality employees.

Interviewing

You can certainly master one or more effective interview techniques; which specific method you choose depends on your organization's culture, your strengths and temperament, and the position in question.[2] You might employ a behavior-based interviewing method for most positions, and a case-study method for more sophisticated jobs. Some groups, especially in technical fields, swear by the "puzzle" interview, in which a candidate must answer a question such as "how many peas would fill Yankee Stadium?" (The objective of the question is to see how the candidate analyzes unanticipated situations or problems).[3] The so-called stress interview is intended to strip away pretense and reveal hidden truths about a candidate. Whichever style (or combination of styles) you choose, individually or as a team, your success hinges on whether you can design job interviews both to determine a candidate's probable behavior at work, and to project your employer brand.

Select and Project

The job interview is a two-way street, and that matters for several reasons.

First, although managers typically regard the interview as their opportunity to select from among several candidates, they forget that the best candidates are also selecting from among several options. If the candidates are employed, they can remain in their current positions. High-demand candidates get approached periodically, and so are comparing several opportunities to yours, including offers they have already declined. Even in transition between jobs, candidates have the option to keep looking.

Second, the onboarding process of a new employee begins long before she actually joins the payroll. Job interviews are a time to set expectations, inform a candidate of resources, and plan early days of the job. This information can make the difference between your offer and your competitors'. (For more on onboarding, see Chapter 9.)

Third, you are marketing your organization at all times, including every job interview. Johnson & Johnson treats everyone it interviews with respect because that projects the employer brand of caring *and* creates advocates among candidates *and*, not incidentally, promotes a brand among customers who buy its products.

Lisa Calicchio, director of recruiting for the Pharmaceuticals Team at Johnson & Johnson, points out that respect includes open sharing of a candidate's chances—and forms a longer relationship.

> Candidates say at the end of the interview, "I just want to know—if I'm moving forward, great. If I'm not, well, I'm sad about that, but just let me know so I can move on." We are as clear as possible about a candidate's status, to the point where we actually tell folks when they're in the second tier. We let them know that we're always leaving room for a future opportunity. Johnson & Johnson gets a lot of candidates who may not be a fit for one job but right for another down the line. So we deliver a balanced message—we can say "not this time" and still keep them engaged.

Finally, an interview process that reflects your values highlights potential conflicts between your personality and that of the candidate. You might be great at projecting a tough, competitive, and individual style, thinking you draw more out of a candidate, but if collaboration is critical to your work, what message are you sending?

The job of the full-time recruiter, from the first phone contact, is to do a very thorough analysis of the *can-do* part—to verify experience and skills—first and quickly. That leaves values, culture, and temperament—the qualities that determine the *will-do* part—for the bulk of the interview process.

Whether a candidate *can do* the job is easier to determine than whether she *will do* the job. The interview process has to determine both.

One of the best executive recruiters we know, Liz Kelleher, asks herself, "Can I be an advocate for this candidate? Only then will I put her forward to management." It's her job to fill that seat; she's got a lot of seats to fill, but she takes the time to develop a relationship with the candidate that goes beyond just checking off skills. She looks for motivations and gets to know what that candidate is like on a personal level. She lays out the process—who the candidate will meet, when, and why—early in the interview process. When a candidate Liz advocates finally appears before the manager, that person tends to be very comfortable and well prepared, which leads to a better interview. This isn't because Liz has coached her—it's because Liz has made the match and decided to advocate because the candidate will work out well.

> *Whether a candidate* can do *the job is easier to determine than whether she* will do *the job. The interview process has to determine both.*

Over time we've learned that if Liz goes to bat for a candidate, that person is probably going to work out. She's not going to send anybody to an executive interview that she wouldn't hire herself.

This is not just for executives; it's particularly good for lower-level employees because they're usually nervous. They're not smooth at interviewing. But they are the future of your organization. A good interviewer puts them at ease so that the hiring manager can get an accurate interview, not one distorted by nervousness.

Here's how several typical questions for a midlevel manager get at the predictive *will do* against one quality of organizational culture—whether individual accomplishment or team effort is more critically required for success or more valued as part of the culture.

How Steve Interviews

"When I have a candidate come in, I don't necessarily launch right into questions. I say the same thing every time: that one of the foundational principles of this company is that the job seeker's in control. I acknowledge to the candidate that she can go to any company ... she can stay in her current job or go work somewhere else. Then I say, 'So rather than me just grilling you, let's have a conversation. I want you to spend as much time asking me questions as I spend asking you.'

"If you bring in a person in and just fire, fire, fire, fire questions without getting the candidate's perspective, or giving him or her time to think and respond, that's a poor reflection of your employer brand.

"We also always ask the receptionist, and my executive assistant Melissa Tremblay, 'What did you think of that person?' It's amazing how many managerial candidates put on a great act for executives but are rude, condescending, or dismissive of staff. It tells us a lot about how they'll treat their people."

—*Steve Pogorzelski, Executive Vice President, Monster.com*

Q: *"You're going to come in and you're going to run this department. Tell me what will your plan be for the first 100 days?"*

A: Does the candidate say, "I'm going to take immediate action, and make sweeping changes?" That approach will work if your organization lionizes individuals and if the candidate is expected to force immediate change. However, that approach would not work in an interdependent environment, a matrix reporting structure, or a customer-focused environment.

The collaborative culture would prefer an answer like "I'm going to take the time to talk to my people on the front lines. I'm going to learn more about the customers."

Q: *"What was your greatest success, and what did you learn?"*

A: How many times does a candidate say the word I instead of we? If it's a lot, you could be talking with a big ego, not a team player. When you ask about a candidate's biggest failure, does he stick with I or does failure become a we event? We like an attitude that says "I'm going to share the success but be personally accountable for failure." It shows that those people are willing to learn from their mistakes. At Monster, you're allowed to make smart mistakes as long as you understand why the mistake happened. Ask the candidate to analyze success and failure: Did you do the homework up front? Why did this mistake happen instead of that one? You can only do that honestly if you take accountability for mistakes—and if the culture rewards that attitude instead of punishing it. That attitude might not work in another culture where teamwork is less important or where personal accountability is secondary.

Q: *What gets you up in the morning? What are you passionate about?*

A: Here's another often-used question that can both select a candidate and project an employer brand, based on the individual versus the team.

   Typically, a response from a candidate will be something like "I like to solve problems, and I like to win." Often that person will include a quality she's culled from your marketing. That's okay—but listen between the words a little, too: in a team-oriented culture, we'd want to hear an answer like "I want to be able to come in and work hard, be highly organized, be effective, and then go home and play with my children" (or practice with my band, or pursue my volunteer work). We believe someone who likes balance is going to be a better team leader. Again, that's a cultural characteristic of

Monster. The organization where a lone wolf succeeds might want to hear the answer "I like to solve problems, I like to win" followed by "my typical day is working until five, hitting the gym, then coming back and working until ten." Not much balance there, but if you're in investment banking or a start-up, that might be just what the culture demands.

Interviewing can also reveal, in subtle signals, the authenticity of a candidate's answers. Ask a manager "what do your subordinates think of you?" and you'll learn a lot by how direct he is about his shortcomings (subordinates always know shortcomings), and you'll also know whether that candidate communicates candidly with his staff. Can he hear criticism from those he manages or is there a strict command-style hierarchy in his style?

Q: *How would you like to grow professionally?*

What opportunities do you see here?

Why would you choose to work here instead of our competition, or the noncompetitive company down the street?

How would you put this job in the context of what this organization is trying to achieve?

A: When you ask questions like these, you're trying to get a candidate to paint a portrait of herself, and in that portrait you'll see the match between her values and yours.

Today, if candidates don't come to an interview knowing a lot about the organization, they're lazy. With the availability of data on the Internet, there's no excuse for ignorance. A great guerilla tactic to find out what a candidate knows is to turn the tables and ask the candidate to interview the manager. Does she discuss specific problems? How does she process new information? Has her research turned up new opportunities? Put the candidate in your place—and be prepared to answer tough questions from the candidate who has done her homework.

Hiring expert Dr. John Sullivan proposed a related reengineering of the interview process this way: "Consider how you would hire a chef (or musician or writer). You certainly wouldn't spend a lot of time talking about knife skills; instead, you would put the candidates in the kitchen and then taste their food. The same would be true for an athlete . . . you'd give him a tryout. It turns out that nothing is a better predictor of on-the-job performance than 'putting them in the kitchen,' even if it's only for a brief period."[4]

Why interview a candidate by asking her to do the job? This is the basis of the "case-study interview" used by business consultancies, universities, and other employers where brainpower and communication skills are critical. Throw a candidate into the real world and see what she does.

Closing the Candidate

The interviews are done, assessments are collected, and you collectively weigh the pros and cons of the top candidates. A decision is made, and it's time to close this candidate, right?

Actually, the time to close this candidate was several steps ago. By the time your decision is made, the ideal candidate should be ready to say yes because she's learned so much through the Attract and Acquire stages that she also knows it's a match. It's just a matter now of closing the deal—that is, coming to terms. There might be some negotiation ahead, some budget checking and further discussion of a position (especially for a senior or leadership role), but if all has gone well, you and the candidate are already close to a mutual decision.

Even the closing offers a chance to validate your employer brand. In the following review, we'll see how checking references, making the offer, negotiation, and onboarding all can set up the organization and new employee for mutual success.

Close with a focus on the tangible and intangible benefits. You don't want a candidate to make a decision just around compensation, which can be easily matched by your competitors. You've got to assume that the candidate has the potential to get other offers (or she has no compelling reason to leave her current job). Even if she's unemployed, tell yourself she'd rather sleep in the car for another two weeks than take the wrong job. Treating the candidate as if she had options is part of treating her like a customer.

Start the close with thoughtful communication. Standard offer letters look like they came from the Internal Revenue Service! "Your salary's this, you'll get three weeks vacation, blah, blah, blah . . ." The implicit assumption is that there's nothing to talk about except numbers—even after an interview process that was an in-depth business conversation. Offer letters (and the calls that precede them) should emphasize shared values, the opportunity for career advancement, the quality of the team, the chance to bring a company to greatness . . . whatever you've seen resonate with the candidate. For example:

> Dear Mary,
>
> We think you're the right person for the job of operations manager at XYZ Company, not only because of the skills you demonstrated in your current job but also because of the deep understanding you showed in our discussions of XYZ's changing operations model. As a family-owned company, we're driven as much by our values as by the bottom line, and your enthusiasm and can-do attitude fit perfectly. Your stated desire to step up from a single contributor to a manager seems to fit as well, and we will be proud to say you learned to manage a staff here at XYZ. With that in mind, we're pleased to offer you a salary of $42,000 per year . . . [etc.]

The boilerplate about salary and benefits can follow the statement that reiterates the value, beyond money, of the person you're taking on.

A letter is only a formality. You and/or the hiring manager should take a "welcome to the team" approach on the phone, in e-mail, or in a face-to-face meeting with the candidate. Show the candidate that you appreciate she's making a big decision, and you want her to feel great about it.

The close is a typical time to check references, but it should have happened earlier. Paul W. Barada, author of *Reference Checking for Everyone*, offers the following high-level view of good reference-checking habits.

First, Check

Absurd as it may seem, many employers don't check references at all. Given the state of the world, it's more important than ever. A recent Monster survey showed 72 percent of employers checked references—and 58 percent of managers said they'd seen job seekers misrepresent their work experience.

Check Everyone

There are employers who check references on some candidates and not on others. This does not mean the scope or comprehensiveness of the check has to be the same for every level or position, but some form of reference checking, appropriate to the position, should be carried out on all candidates.

MY POV

"If I know that there's another offer on the table that might be a bit better than ours, I'll enlist the managers to convince this person that we really want him. The manager will call him directly and say, 'Hey listen, I know that you spoke with Kelly, and she made you the offer. Do you have any questions about any of that? I want to reiterate the fact that we were very excited about the possibility of you starting with us. We recognize that you have tons of potential to advance here—more than at other places.' They keep the dialogue going with specifics about the job, and often the candidate will accept the job in the end. The manager has listened and convinced him that he's our type of person. He sees the upside that another job won't give him, even for a few dollars more."

—Kelly Hogan, Eze Castle Software

Check References Before You're Ready to Make an Offer

References should be checked much earlier in the process than when many employers actually perform them. Once the top two or three candidates have been identified through résumé screenings and initial interviews, references should be checked before any consideration is given to making a job offer. If the references confirm a candidate's skills, experience, and ability, then conduct a follow-up interview armed with that knowledge. More importantly, making an offer contingent on a positive reference check creates a legal relationship between the employer and the candidate.

Require References from People Who Have Worked Directly with the Candidate

Employers have every right to ask candidates to provide a list of the types of references they want, not just the ones the candidate wants them to have. Insist that candidates provide the names of at least one former supervisor, a peer, and a subordinate (if they've managed anyone). Talk with people who have actually worked with the candidate on a daily basis within the last five to seven years.

Ask References Open-Ended Questions and Follow Up

Refrain from yes-or-no questions. Instead of asking, "Was Bill a good worker?" you should ask, "How would you describe Bill's on-the-job performance?" Then follow up. If a reference says Sue was the best employee the company ever had, ask, "Could you tell me how her performance was so extraordinary?"

Reference checking requires time, training, and tact. If done properly, it can be one of the most useful hiring tools available to any employer. If done poorly, it can lead to hiring someone who not only can't do the job but also who could do more harm than good for the company.

Simple behaviors at this time project your professionalism:

- **Close candidates quickly.** Slow decision making puts off candidates who are in demand and increases the probability of them getting multiple simultaneous offers.
- **Stay in touch.** If you experience any delay in making an offer, tell the candidate immediately. Not only does this show your desire to bring that person on board, but it sets up an expectation that the candidate will also respond quickly and inform you of any delay in his or her decision.

Negotiating the Deal

Negotiation is a matter of corporate business methods and culture, and it's not our purpose to provide a primer of deal-making tips (you'll find sources for this in the Resources section beginning on page 215). You land candidates with a deal that confirms their worth, satisfies your budget, and leaves both sides ready to do business—in short, by building a win-win deal. How flexible you can be, and how complex the deal is, depends on the importance of the role as well as issues of fairness. But by the time you get to the offer stage, the outlines of a deal should be clear to both parties. If the offer is way off base, someone hasn't done the necessary homework.

Candidates are more sensitive about this process than any other in the Acquire stage, so your behavior is under close, often emotional scrutiny. Is the negotiation oppositional, or are you clearly looking for a mutually beneficial deal? Who does the negotiating—a single person in human resources or the candidate's future manager? On what terms are you flexible, and what is non-negotiable in your culture? What is your strategy for handling a candidate who has multiple offers? Will you offer intangible benefits (for example, work-at-home arrangements) in lieu of higher pay? By what measures will you know you've made a good deal today and a year from now?

Your negotiation style makes a big impression on a candidate. Candidates will promote a good experience and spread the word just as rapidly about a poor one. If your version of negotiation is "take it or leave it," you're putting yourself at risk of losing the candidate either at this point or six months later when a better offer comes knocking at her door. On the contrary, a respectful negotiation, in mutual understanding, continues the business relationship you want with a keeper and improves retention later.

This is the beginning of onboarding, a priceless practice that we'll discuss in detail in Chapter 9. For the purpose of closing the candidate, you might begin onboarding even before you're completely closed (even just for symbolic value). Before a candidate says yes, have her meet a mentor or buddy. Describe the process the candidate will engage in when she starts in the new job. Have her join in the planning. The candidate should have met as many players as possible at this point—managers and staff, of course, but also those others we described earlier, such as members of related departments or internal service groups. You want to move the candidate's conception of working with you from imagination to anticipation, because then she is more likely to say yes.

Review

- Every step along the "funnel" is an opportunity to capture the best candidate's interest and build relationships with future prospects.
- The interview process is a two-way conversation, and even small improvements differentiate your employer brand from your competitors'.
- Hiring managers, whatever their expertise, must learn fundamentals of effective interviewing and carry the employer branding message through the interview.
- Use candidate assessments to help choose candidates and to improve the quality of dialogue during interviews.
- Closing begins early in the process and should carry a consistent message with your employer brand. Be particularly alert to reinforcing the intangible benefits of working for your organization when making the job offer.

Chapter 9

Hire and Hold: Retention

Retention—holding on to the talented employees you worked so hard to attract and acquire—is the third phase of the Engagement Cycle and one of the make-or-break issues for companies today. In a recent Monster study, 70 percent of organizations listed workforce retention as a primary concern for the business. It has a direct effect on company performance. Brian D. Lowenthal of Benchmark Partners notes that top-performing companies have first-year turnover rates of 5 percent or less.[1] If you're among those 70 percent and not doing everything you can to hold on to your keepers, you're spending too much time recruiting and not enough retaining.

The tenure situation might be worse than organizations realize, because there's a strong difference in expectations between management and employees. Our research shows that while most hiring managers and staffing directors expect employees to remain longer than three to five years, most new employ-ees anticipate staying only one to three years.[2]

Retention is the decisive test of good hiring. You can convince yourself that employees are loyal, but during a skills shortage in any business, other compa-nies recruit poised employees with high-value skills. They're offered more money, responsibility, and/or status. The poised employee needs reasons to stay, and once again, our research finds a disconnect between what employees think and what their employers believe employees think. Employers believe that retention is ultimately a money chase, with salaries rising in response to talent shortages—classic wage inflation.

Our research reveals a more complex picture than that. Salary and benefits are important, but an employee's feeling of attachment comes from such intan-gible rewards as pride in the organization or a belief that both leadership and his manager cares personally about his welfare. It's intangible promises like the prospect of professional growth that stimulate a sense of belonging.

It turns out that loyalty is largely inspired by the same intangible rewards that attracted someone to a firm in the first place. This is especially good news for smaller companies, which cannot compete on salary alone but which can complete on the employment experience to hire and hold the best.

Earlier, we discussed how an effective employer brand strategy has to be an authentic reflection of the workplace for recruiting. This is pertinent to retention as well: Make the workplace an embodiment of the employer brand and you'll hold on to those people you attracted. You'll create a virtuous cycle of employee satisfaction that in turn validates the employer brand to the outside world.

We'll spell out several initiatives to help retention, but first, let's look at the true cost of turnover.

The Cost of Turnover

Only one-third of HR managers say they actually calculate what an employee's voluntary departure costs their company. More cite out-of-pocket costs such as advertising and recruitment fees to replace an employee, but these costs understate turnover's full impact.

Knowing the full cost of replacing an employee is especially important during times of low unemployment, when talent is in demand and more people are willing to switch jobs, and recruiters spend time and money just to stop the bleeding. Turnover takes more of a recruitment budget than you might think. In 2006, for example, it accounted for 28 to 35 percent of online job postings. Turnover like that means a company with 200 employees that plans to grow its workforce by 10 percent *and* compensate for losing 30 percent of its current workforce has to hire not 20 people this year but 80. Just replacing people who leave consumes a huge amount of recruitment resources!

But wait. It gets worse.

The larger cost of valuable employees leaving is lost productivity. The gap between the times a skilled worker leaves and the time his replacement is up to speed is a money vacuum. It takes time for the replacement to ramp up to acceptable performance, and longer for productive, profitable work to match the former employee's level. The time, shown in Figure 9-1, can be a few weeks or (for high-level positions) many months.[3]

Figure 9-1

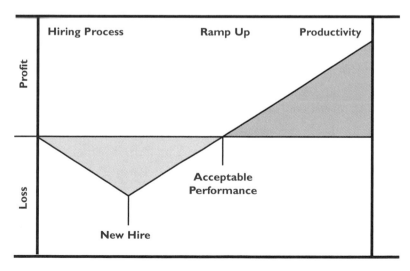

There are at least four categories of costs, and only one of savings, after a voluntary departure, and when you add them up it looks like this:

A. Cost of acquisition (advertising, recruiter time, manager interviewing time, legal and nonsalary compensation, reference checks, background check, raises, etc.).

PLUS

B. Cost of replacement setup (training, IT setup, benefits setup, etc.)

PLUS

C. Cost of lost productivity during gap before replacement starts

PLUS

D. Cost of lost productivity until replacement reaches lost employee's productivity level.

MINUS

E. Lost employee's unpaid compensation during gap before replacement starts

$$A + B + C + D - E = \text{Cost of replacement}$$

Here's a back-of-the-envelope calculation: a midlevel accounts receivable manager, making $60,000 per year, leaves and is replaced in three weeks. What does that cost?

A = $400 job ad; $1,200 recruiter time; $1,500 raise; $1,000 fees = **$4,100**

B = **$1,250**

C = Manager is not replaceable with temporary worker, so the work is divided between two employees, who each become 40 percent less productive for three weeks at a salary of $52,000 = **$2,400**

D = The replacement takes 90 days to reach productivity level of earlier manager, with the gap averaging 25 percent = **$3,750**

E = **$3,461**

SIMPLE COST OF REPLACEMENT: **$8,039**

That's 13.4 percent of a $60,000 salary; in fact, this is a conservative esti-mate[4] because it's still only a high-level view. To calculate the full cost of this par-ticular financial opening, you'd factor in items like the delay in collecting money owed the company, interest not earned on that money, time others in the depart-ment spend interviewing replacements, interrupted work, canceled meetings, and stalled projects. There are hidden costs throughout, and they rise with a job's complexity and interdependence with other positions. Expert studies put the full cost of replacement between 30 percent of annual salary for hourly workers and 150 percent for executive positions.[5]

But wait. It gets even worse.

Even harder to calculate is the opportunity cost of losing a keeper. When a sales representative leaves, the opportunity cost includes lost sales that employee would have made during the time it takes for a replacement to get up to speed. It includes the loss of all the relationships and goodwill that sales rep has earned with customers. When an innovative designer or product manager leaves, the potential revenue from that person's products is lost. And don't forget the lost knowledge, the lost leadership capacity, and even an employee's contribution to a good workplace experience for others. Is it any wonder organizations that truly measure turnover are doing everything they can to decrease it?

Calculating the business impact of turnover enables you to consider what an appropriate investment should be to keep employees. It's similar to the cal-culations made in the retail industry that prove investing in existing customer relationships is cheaper than acquiring new customers.

Turnover analysis can also uncover the strengths and shortcomings of man-agers over time as you keep track of who has left the organization and why. Say, for example, that you notice a high turnover rate in groups reporting to one manager and that that manager rates most of his male employees A-level per-formers and all of his female employees C-level. The women are leaving—is that a hiring problem or an attitude problem? Are the ratings fair, or has the turnover in female employees pointed out a problem with the manager?

With such analytical insight, managers are in a better position to take a "cost of doing business" expense, to which recruitment is unfortunately often relegated, and elevate it to support a strategic cause.

Learn Why People Leave

When we hear managers wondering about turnover, we ask if they really understand the reasons people leave.

When people leave voluntarily, they don't want to burn bridges, so they say they're leaving for more money. No argument with that, right? The problem is, most of the time it's only part of the story.

When independent researchers ask why people leave, money is rarely the dominant reason. Studies done by the Gallup Organization, the Saratoga Institute, and Monster cite a poor relationship with the boss as a main reason an employee leaves. It breaks the bond he might have with even a great job. Beverly Kaye and Sharon Jordon-Evans, authors of *Love 'em or Lose 'em*, say exciting work, career growth, great colleagues, and good bosses are top reasons people stay; the opposite—boring work, stagnation, a bad environment, and lousy bosses—are reasons people leave. Employers who discover the specific reasons good people leave can fix those problems much faster and add reasons to stay.

> *If you don't know why people are leaving you probably don't know the real reasons they're staying, either.*

If you don't know why people are leaving you probably don't know the real reasons they're staying, either. This is as much about management being out of touch as it is about the mindset of the poised worker. Remember that you can learn a lot just walking the floor every few days and talking to employees about their work and their lives. Not every answer is found in a formal employee survey.

Actually, exit interviews *can* help when you get beyond the money talk, but you need a special relationship to break through that barrier. You can have a third party do your exit interviews. You can have a trusted peer do them, or designate the right person as an "ombudsman" for departing employees, whose task is to interview deeply and find patterns. This person not only asks "why are you leaving?" but also "what about your job, or manager, or this company, made you receptive to another offer?" The exit interviewer also asks "what attracted you to this company in the first place? were your expectations met?" The exit interviewer gets details about the employee's first six months on the job, when impressions are strongly formed. He probes the relationship with the departing employee's boss, senior management, and the company's employer brand. The exit interviewer returns fearlessly and confidentially to the subject of the employee's relationship to his manager, upper management, and staff.

There isn't a single number that proves that your turnover rate is acceptable, because the causes are multidimensional. Consider the factors that combine to create turnover:

- The state of the local economy
- Demand for particular jobs
- Quality of managers
- Quality of hiring
- Willingness of competitors to pay more
- Job pressure and stress
- Health of your particular business
- Personal reasons for individuals

Some jobs have built-in turnover. There's a lot of churn in them, as equally skilled people cycle through the job and either move up or move on. We call this phenomenon *churnover*.

Retail managers typically expect some churnover. They'll say, "You're a stocker, or a student, working as a cashier . . . I'm not concerned when you decide to leave. That's churnover, and it's a pain but it doesn't hit my bottom line. But if you're the brilliant merchandise buyer who knows what customers want, I have a problem when a competitor steals you. That's turnover."

Accepting churnover is part of directing more of your time and money to the highest-value employees—in other words, the keepers who will deliver the greatest profit to your business.

What You Can Learn from Loyalists

One good step: turn to your longtime employees and ask why they are still with you. Those who have developed a loyalty to your organization can tell you what you're doing right.

Although most employees embrace the poised mindset we described in Chapter 2, the 30 percent who describe themselves as loyalists have much to teach us about holding on to those poised workers. By understanding the attitudes of loyal workers, employers can develop strategies to retain the talent that exists within their company.

Employees naturally compare their workplace with others, past and potential, and if you are better by comparison, you can raise the emotional "barrier to exit" among your skilled workers. Monster's study of loyal workers in 2006 uncovered several factors that are important to the A-level loyalists, which an employer can use to encourage top players to stay. Our key findings about the attitudes of loyalists toward their work, boss, company, and compensation include

- Loyalists perceive their work as challenging, interesting, and personally fulfilling.
- Loyalists have strong relationships with their boss, transcending beyond that of supervisor/subordinate.
- Loyalists are clear about what their boss expects of them.
- Loyalists maintain a good work-life balance, and their bosses support their personal lives.
- Loyalists believe their company is a good place to work and are proud of their company.
- Loyalists view compensation as an important factor in their loyalty.

Armed with this knowledge, any employer can utilize strategies to better manage, develop, and retain loyal workers. Consider the following when developing hire-and-hold strategies:

- Promote the full value of a worker's compensation, not just salary. This includes highlighting the costs associated with benefits such as health insurance and pension plans. Train managers to personally encourage workers to use every possible benefit.

• Monitor worker sentiment closely and continuously, and measure it to keep a pulse on worker attitudes. Develop proactive strategies to manage significant changes. Worker loyalty, like the work environment, is fluid. Don't assume last year's loyalty carried over through this year's events.

• Worker loyalty is dynamic; it's not an inherent personality trait. A loyal worker can become disenchanted with his or her company, boss, or compensation at any time. Changes that might impact a worker's perception of his or her job should be taken into consideration in advance.

• A company's reputation is an important factor in employee retention, as indicated by the pride exhibited by loyal workers. Employers should be sure to promote their contributions and value to the community, through both their products and philanthropy.

• Good managers who communicate well, set clear expectations, and promote a healthy work-life balance make loyal workers.

• Leverage loyalists as advocates whenever possible when recruiting (bring them in to interviews to talk up the company).

Loyalty is a point of view about one's employer, but even the 70 percent of workers who describe themselves as poised can feel a stronger bond with their work situation. There is another, even more powerful state of mind that encourages both greater productivity and greater retention, and that is keeping the employed engaged in his work.

Employee Engagement

To this point, we've used the term *engagement* in terms of the Engagement Cycle—the relationship of a candidate or employee with a company throughout the Attract, Acquire, and Advance phases. For a moment, let's talk about employee engagement in a somewhat different sense: a strong attachment to the work itself.

The Gallup Organization, management consultants Towers Perrin, and others have conducted extensive research that confirms what you know in your gut: people who are deeply engaged in their work are happier and more bonded to their employer.

Researchers use the term *discretionary effort* to describe the behaviors that accompany engagement. We see employee engagement as both an attachment to the work at hand and a drive for growth, achievement, and going beyond "reasonable" goals based on inner psychological reward. We see it in the team that stays up all night to solve a problem, the boss who postpones an important meeting to be with an employee facing a personal crisis, and the entry-level worker who stays late studying to increase his skills not because he's being paid but just because he loves the work.

Skilled workers who are engaged in their work are closer to the customer, the goals, and the personal rewards simply because those are the active players in the ecosystem of work.

Engagement is also profitable. In a 2006 survey of 664,000 employees worldwide, the research firm ISR found profound gaps between companies with highly engaged employees and those with low engagement scores:

On Operating Income:

Engaged = 19.2 percent gain; Nonengaged = 32.7 percent decline

On Net Income Growth:

Engaged = 13.2 percent gain; Nonengaged = 3.8 percent decline

On Earnings per Share:

Engaged = 27.8 percent gain; Nonengaged = 11.2 percent decline

An engaged workforce clearly contributes to the bottom line, and managers build the road to engagement one employee at a time. It comes down to managers transcending the typical supervisor-employee relationship with that full set of retention-focused practices in their daily management.

Turnover, loyalty, and engagement—so much about retention has to do with hiring the right people in the first place. If your employer brand reflects your organization, you attract and acquire people who buy into what the company's trying to do. You attract people who share your values and believe in your mission. Early in the process, it's not a matter of hiring people and then engaging them—it's a matter of hiring engaged people and then managing toward that sense of engagement.

Great companies get this, and tailor engagement to their core values. Google encourages virtual teams to form around new products someone just dreamed up—after hiring creative people. Wegmans encourages people to find new ways to delight customers—after hiring people who are customer-focused.

In Chapter 5, we said the employer brand embodies the day-to-day experience of working at an organization. Now think about how this applies to each employee and either encourages or discourages engagement: if your brand says everyone's voice matters, then your managers must learn to listen actively, engaging each employee in a real back-and-forth of ideas. If an employee brainstorms an idea at 3 a.m., then rushes in early to discuss it with his manager, that manager had better shut down his e-mail for 20 minutes and encourage the employee to describe the idea. If the response instead is "write down that idea and I'll get to it later," how engaged will that employee remain?

If your employer brand says the company is open, honest, and direct about resolving conflicts, then managers must develop a tolerance for criticism and encourage debate among their staffs. They should discourage backroom politics and reward transparency in decision making.

Engagement is about passion, which comes from within, and managers nurture engagement when they reward that passion and remove roadblocks. Whatever an employee was hired to do, from driving a forklift to negotiating a billion-dollar acquisition, the passion that makes that person want to do more than the job description propels engagement. When managers authentically live the employer brand principles that attracted that passion in the first place, they're creating fertile ground for engagement.

Hiring for retention also means conforming individual career aspirations and your ability to deliver on those aspirations. If you don't have a career ladder to climb, you have to make sure you're not hiring somebody who's going to gauge his success or contribution by getting that promotion every three years.

Compensation

Most candidates naturally admit that compensation in all its forms (money, benefits, stock, paid time off, etc.) is the number one inducement to take a new job. It's obviously also a motivator for staying in a job or for leaving it.

Most experienced managers have had a talented employee approach them and say, "I've been offered more money elsewhere, but I'd like to stay." The market has spoken, the person has indicated a willingness to leave . . . and the manager has a choice. Assuming he wants to retain the employee, the manager can:

- Match the competitor's offer; this should be done if the offer is demonstrably within the market and doesn't create parity issues with other employees (if everyone is underpaid, you have a more serious problem).
- Work with the employee to find an equivalent reason to stay—an accelerated promotion, greater participation in other forms of compensation, and so on, based on the employee's performance.

Whatever the outcome, this is an opportunity to learn about the employment experience. At Monster, we always ask "why would you want to leave?" and also "why would you want to stay?" (as opposed to "what can I do to make you stay?"—the difference is important). The answers tell you the importance of compensation relative to the intangible rewards of working at the company.

Recruiter Terry Frugoli remembers how he learned that a money question was about a lot more than just money and turned it into a retention opportunity.

I was working for OmniVision Technologies at a time when competition for software specialists was keen. I found out a talented software engineer—a Ph.D. in image sensor technology—was looking for work after just a few months on the job, and asked him in confidence, "What's going on?" He said, "To be honest, the last job blindsided me with a layoff, so I'm feeling pretty insecure." Then he said, "Other companies have offered me a little more money, too." He was being completely honest.

So I went to his director, and explained the situation. He said, "We don't want him to leave. Maybe we can move up his salary review and send him a message . . . if it means he'll stay."

Then I went back to the engineer and said, "Your director definitely does not want you to leave, and this is what we're going to do to make sure you know how serious he is about your future here . . ." He looked at me, surprised, and he said, "You know, I've never had anybody take that much interest in keeping me in a company. It really makes me feel wanted." We shook hands, and he's still here, several years later.

Delayed compensation like bonuses, stock awards, and pension or retirement plan contributions is meant to induce people to stay when they're at top performance, but it also provides intangible benefits, says compensation consultant Tom Wilson. "What does it mean to somebody when they actually receive a bonus, stock, profit sharing, or some other form of equity?" he asks. "It means they are a part of the club, they're special. Stories of start-up millionaires notwithstanding, most company equity doesn't result in huge payoffs. There's certainly a monetary reward, but not so great that other companies can't match it to land a great midlevel employee. The symbolic importance might be more important for retention than the actual cash value."

For the purpose of retention, it's important to note that particular forms of compensation come and go with the times. Stock options had great cachet in the 1990s until the bubble burst. Filling retirement funds with company stock seemed great until Enron and others went bust.

Today, employees want robust health and medical benefits. In Monster's 2007 survey,[6] 64 percent of employees in the United States rated health insurance as the most important benefit, and 82 percent rated it at least "highly valuable," yet only 22 percent of employers offer free health insurance, and just 42 percent offer subsidized insurance. Health-care costs are hitting the bottom line hard for both employees and employers, but clearly there is a disconnect between employer and employee on the issue, and aggressive companies can view health care as an opportunity to gain a competitive advantage by delivering superior health-care benefits. The report indicates that such a cost may be offset by better retention rates and decreased hiring costs.

The same research shows that long-term, conservative, and reliable monetary benefits such as competitive 401(k) and pension plans are highly appealing to employees when they look at total compensation packages. Employers show a strong preference for annual performance-based bonuses, tying greater compensation more closely to today's results.[7]

Hold Supervisors Accountable

Supervisors are in the best position to directly influence employee morale and other attributes that ultimately determine employee retention. In earlier chapters, we said they are in a prime position to help hire the best, and here we'll add that they are by far the most important factor when it comes to holding the best.

Only 11 percent of firms surveyed by Monster report having managers' compensation tied to employee retention.[8] Yet managers are the strongest levers for reducing turnover, and so firms with a corporate objective of reducing turnover have to do it at the manager level.

The fastest way to hold managers accountable for retention of staff is in their pay. Some percentage of a supervisor's bonus should be tied to retention goals. Turnover rates have to be held to a number agreed upon in advance, in concert with other business goals (the number comes from a baseline of last year's turnover or current industry and regional benchmarks). You want to see year-to-year improvement in turnover overall, but you especially want to see a percentage of A-level performers retained. Bonuses for low turnover should be offered to managers at all levels, weighted so you give a little more for holding on to A-level players. If you drive this objective down through all your organization, you make people more vested in the hiring process. You also have to empower these managers to affect retention beyond hiring people who are a good fit. Train supervisors to become more aware of the cost of turnover, the value of worker retention, and ways to hold on to the winners.

Exercise

Here's an interesting exercise for the Chief Financial Officer (CFO): compare the cost of turnover to the cost of offering better health-care benefits. If a better health-care plan decreased turnover by, say, 10 percent, would it pay for itself?

A Retention Practice

Here are the general initiatives our research found in workplaces that encourage people to stay.

Deliver a Balanced Workplace

When the demands of their jobs conflict with the satisfaction of their personal lives, employees struggle and are more inclined to leave. It's a worldwide problem, especially as cities become more congested, commutes become longer, and more two-career families cope with packed schedules. Companies that recognize work-life balance issues can help employees feel personal satisfaction while meeting the company objectives.

Senior managers are growing more supportive and even forceful in promoting work-life balance. In fact, one CEO we encountered in our research routinely calls senior managers to discuss their work habits when he feels they are working too much.

Balance is about more than getting away from the office. Fifty-five percent of HR managers report offering their employees social activities, and about 15

Benefits that Balance Work

There are dozens of ways to promote a balanced workplace for your employees. For employees seeking balance, small stuff matters—services and considerations that save time or a little money for your employees. For example:

- BEA Systems has an auto detailer visit its campus so that employees can care for their cars without having to spend personal time with this chore.
- Google offers its employees on-site dry cleaning, haircuts, and coin-free laundry rooms at its main campus.
- Italian food company Ferrero offers free pediatric care for employees with children aged from birth to 14 years, in addition to the services provided by the national health service.
- Jet Blue's 800-plus reservation agents all work from their home offices. The company reports that agent retention is well above the industry average while agents have become 25 percent more productive.
- In the United Kingdom, retailer J. Sainsbury and the shop workers union created a financial arrangement whereby older workers can reduce weekly working hours with no loss of pay, drawing on pension benefits.[9]

percent offer employee sports leagues. These types of social events enable workers to create the social bonds that emotionally tie them to their work and employer. They also demonstrate to potential employees the value a company places on personal fulfillment, which can dramatically differentiate one company from another during the recruiting process.

Proactively Manage Succession

A growing number of HR managers are now focused on succession planning as a means to reduce worker turnover. If employees know they're working toward a more rewarding position, they're more likely to stay. Good planning carries the additional benefit of easing transition from an experienced manager to his successor.

To ensure that employees know what to expect and what is expected of them, both human resources and managers should promote inclusive succession plans that prepare each employee for a two-year business cycle. Employees learn in detail how they will be compensated as a result of achievements. Succession planning can free high achievers from distracting thoughts of compensation and advancement and ease the temptation to move on. They can prevent the mutual shock of hiring outsiders to enter the organization at a high level by grooming people from the inside to take senior positions.

Stay Connected Through Multiple Channels

An employee departure that comes as a surprise represents a breakdown in communication ("who knew he was unhappy?") and the best managers we know keep close to the individuals reporting to them and the larger mood of the company. This is as simple as really listening, asking the right questions, becoming interested in a key employee's hopes, ambitions, enthusiasms, and concerns . . . but everyone communicates a little differently. It means hallway conversations, closed-door confidences, e-mail and voicemail, and walking around. It means checking in when something looks wrong and celebrating when something goes right. It means strong onboarding initiatives (see "Onboarding" later in this chapter). Managing multiple channels of communication like this is time consuming, but how else are you going to know what they want?

Organizations with very clear measures, very clear incentive plans, and very clear rewards tend to celebrate victories. Sure, people look forward to the payout, but an open celebration of a great year is a bonding experience for groups, just as small rewards for going the extra mile are bonding experiences for individuals. It raises the barrier to leaving.

Long tenure and the some of its milestones—sticking with the team through hard times, reinventing one's job, lateral movement across departments—should be celebrated, broadcast, and shouted to the rooftops. A recent Monster Intelligence research project discovered that only one-third of employers recognize workers' tenure, but if you don't value staying with the company, who will?

On a companywide level, new survey technologies are enabling companies to persistently monitor employee morale at an affordable cost throughout the employee lifecycle. Having a real-time and continuous practice to monitor employees' sentiments regarding their jobs helps employers correct problems before a crisis appears. With this insight, company managers now have better and fresher information that they need to effectively manage turnover.[10]

Jennifer Tracy of Limited Brands takes a classic marketing message approach: repeating a consistent message. "Employment branding has to continue through the life cycle of the employee . . . and one of the best times is the annual benefits sign-up. That same employment branding message has got to be reinforced just as it was when a person applied for the job, because if you're trying to change the culture of a company through employment branding then you need to make sure that all the messages, external and internal, align. Otherwise you have a confused employee base."

Reward Internal Mobility

Here's a classic bad management scenario: an employee tells a manager that he wants to move to a bigger opportunity internally. The manager replies, "Sure, but now I know you're not interested in the job you have." The manager writes the employee off, and eventually that person leaves. Other employees learn it's safer to leave the company than to show ambition.

Instead, train managers to think holistically about the company and its keepers. Publicly reward managers who grow their people into new jobs, especially in different departments or disciplines. Give them extra recruiting resources to replace internal transfers out of their groups.

Internal candidates hit the ground running and share knowledge across disciplines. Internal candidates are motivated. They have known strengths and weaknesses. They confirm inside and out that ambition and hard work are rewarded—a great attribute of a strong employer brand.

The employee who raises his hand is poised; send a message to the other 70 percent of your workforce that is poised: you want them to stick around.

Internationally, the differences in retention practices are minor. It can be a challenge to engage people away from the home country, and sometimes your employment culture weakens as it goes through the filter of another work culture . . . but overcoming that is a matter of effort, not reinventing yourself in another country. We noted that in countries with a different current work culture generally, such as India today, you might have to adjust your expectations about an acceptable level of turnover, because right now turnover is higher across the board in India (see Chapter 10).

A European manager doing business in Asia might need to adjust his personal style toward behaviors that recognize a worker's status, or adjust a reward system to include greater emphasis on prestigious work locations and less emphasis on long-term equity participation. This is all the more reason to cultivate local talent in recruiting so that you'll know what expectations should be. In areas with higher unemployment it will be easier to retain talent . . . for now.

Emerging markets, such as newly developing countries, deserve a special note here. Sometimes retention is encouraged by easy things, like a clean, safe workplace, but most of the time it's the harder stuff that takes some effort, such as developing stronger relationships between supervisors and people who are doing the work, or mentoring young people. That's especially hard in a high-growth environment (like today's rapidly industrializing countries), because everyone's stretched thin. But that's the kind of thing that helps to get people more connected and engaged with the organization.

The same basic principles hold: respect, recognition, and responsiveness are valued everywhere. Your turnover might still be higher than you have in some other markets, but you can probably put a pretty big dent in the number.

Seven Rules for Retention

1. Make supervisors more accountable for worker retention by tying their compensation to retention performance.
2. Offer a workplace that respects, encourages, and enables a work-life balance.
3. Create proactive succession planning that facilitates career-pathing for top performers.
4. Provide tools to better monitor employee sentiment throughout the employee life cycle.
5. Focus retention efforts and resources on the most talented and highest potential workers.
6. Produce an employment brand "experience" that satisfies workers on multiple levels.
7. Reward internal mobility with an internal free-agent system that enables employees to move freely and without negative consequences from one department to another.

Onboarding

All employees create a personal curve of achievement. Some get off to a fast start and then falter. Some get up to speed at a good pace and still have the resources to build momentum. They engage the organization in a virtuous cycle of productivity and personal growth. Getting off to the right start, as opposed to just a fast start, can make the difference.

Over 75 percent of top-performing companies put new hires through a formal onboarding process.[11] The process takes many forms—classes, activities with departmental and cross-company colleagues, online and written information, and more—and is *experiential*. People learn their jobs largely by doing, and they learn the best ways to be effective in a company largely by doing as well. A formal process, moreover, assures that consistent information spreads through the organization. For this reason, getting current employees engaged in the onboarding process for new hires reinforces your employer brand with existing staff.

You're actually still in the Acquire stage of hiring. You've worked hard to land a talented employee, and that person is with your organization but not fully of your organization. Engagement is the goal now. Fortunately, in the early days, a new employee is immersed in all the reasons he took the job—and a good onboarding experience confirms those reasons.

Monster and Benchmark Partners created a five-step outline for a strong onboarding experience, one that engages the new employee closely with the organization, monitors progress, and helps form the bonds of trust that are the cornerstone of retention. Build a formal onboarding program on this foundation.

Stage 1: First Week, First Impressions

Have a workstation ready with the tools needed to do the job. (It's amazing how often this doesn't happen.) Get the paperwork out of the way. Introduce the new employee to the team, tour the facilities, and review procedures. Reinforce the job interview and decision process by reviewing short- and long-term goals of the job. Educate new hires on the organization's mission, values, and history. Have a senior leader talk about strategy and market factors like the competitive environment. Assign a buddy in the department and a mentor outside the department— that person's job is to answer questions quickly and in confidence.

Note: Hiring managers and recruiters— this is the best time to get feedback on the recruiting process. Ask "what persuaded you to come here?" and "what would you improve in the hiring process?"

Stage 2: Getting Acquainted and Avoiding Buyer's Regret (the First 30 days)

In the first month, new hires should learn their roles and responsibilities in the context of real projects, problems, and activities (as opposed to the job interview). They need to spend time with a manager as well as contacts and leaders of other groups with whom they work. This is the best time to learn important procedures (such as filing expenses) and work-related technologies.

It is also a good time to create a habit of "walking around"—networking informally across the company to understand the big picture. An assigned mentor can introduce the new employee to other groups. Contact with senior leaders in one-on-one or group settings can form a stronger bond to the bigger vision. Strong bonding to a single manager is great but risky in terms of retention . . . if that manager leaves. The mentor should also ask these questions at the two-week mark:

- Were there a desk, computer, and phone for you (or keys to the loading dock, or gas in the hedge trimmer, or whatever else you needed)?
- Could you be effective on day one?
- Does your boss communicate with you?
- Is this the job for which you thought you signed up?
- What concerns do you have?
- Are there any obvious gaps in your knowledge?

Stage 3: Settling In (90 Days)

Orientation is over. This is now a time to log a few concrete achievements, and onboarding shifts focus from giving information to giving feedback. How effectively is the new employee working? What's the relationship with the manager? (Both the manager and mentor should ask this question.) If the new employee is a leader, has he established credibility with other leaders?

Stage 4: Adjusting (Six Months)

Although the sense of "newness" recedes, the new employee is still developing cross-functional relationships and should by this time be a full-fledged member of the group. The employee and manager should be able to describe their relationship in similar terms, and describe similar goals and expectations. The employee should have received regular performance feedback and begun a development/

growth plan. It is an excellent time to check engagement (see "Employee Engagement") and commitment to company goals, values, and strategy.

Stage 5: Fully Engaged

At the one-year mark, you should be measuring the new hire's level of achievement and/or engagement with leadership, culture, work-life balance, work satisfaction, work relationships, personal growth, and the values expressed in your employer brand. Dissatisfaction with one or more of these factors puts an employee at risk of leaving.

Onboarding people in a leadership role follows much the same pattern, with the important difference being that leaders are often winning the engagement of others. Leaders need a few early wins, and a lot of listening to judge the cultural, informational, political, and market forces that will determine their success. To retain leaders at the highest levels is a measure of their success at achieving stated goals, but they aren't all-powerful or all-seeing, and their onboarding requires an active and trustworthy feedback mechanism. Losing a leader, like losing a talented employee at any level, indicates a failure of the system that attracts, acquires, and advances talented individuals.

Getting off to the right start will not guarantee long tenure, but getting off to the wrong start is a waste of time, money, and talent.

Staying On

When we talk about Advance as the third stage of the hiring cycle, it means that you integrate that person into your company, into your "tribal learning" and your formal knowledge management systems. The new employee develops an affinity with the organization. He becomes a contributor. If the match is good, he's inclined to stay.

Then what? The employee, a member of your organization's community, continues to advance in knowledge and contribution. Over time, he grows in both productivity and value. This makes him more valuable to you and to the marketplace seeking talent, and so the question appears pretty quickly—what are you doing to keep him engaged? Retention that flows organically from an affinity for the organization is better than retention bought only with more money, power, or goodies.

"Advance" doesn't always have to be a horizontal ladder of promotion. Not everybody moves up forever, and besides, modern organizations don't work that way. Look at a typical company with a majority of people in sales, customer service, or marketing; those people have only one or two rungs they can climb. Still, the longer they stay and the more you train them both in formal skills and in tribal learning, the more productive they become. The productivity growth of a new salesperson after six months goes up 20 to 30 percent. (Sales is an easy place to see the correlation between increased productivity and increased monetary reward for both the employee and the company.) So they're advancing the company as they advance in their knowledge, their training, and their tenure with the company.

Advance is fundamentally a story of productivity growth. As an employee's skills and knowledge grows, your payoff is in terms of increased productivity and profits. Her personal payoff is increased value in the marketplace. At least, that's one part of her payoff. The rest of the story, if she is in the right career, is that she is using her talents, knowledge, and values more fully. She is contributing to a mission that she believes in, and she is bonded to a community of like-minded people. That bonding—again, the foundation of retention—is worth more than a 5 percent raise to switch jobs. And so, your guidance and methods to advance your best talent, in order to keep it, must be focused on the individual's best career path.

Career paths today look more like latticework than a ladder, as people shift job descriptions, move across departmental lines, pick up a new set of skills while relying on the strengths that made them talented in their last position, and reap multiple rewards. They make more money. They gain more flexibility. They take on new challenges. They get out of a rut and revive the excitement they knew years before when work was new.

We know a scientific devices company that even advances its retirees by bringing them back in mentoring roles. Rather than lose the institutional knowledge and political acumen at gold-watch time, the company transfers retirees to an entirely new role in which they nurture younger employees. Here's a typical story: a "retired" engineer is now training young people, part time. He's still earning, but at the same time, he's spending much more time with his family. He's become a docent at a museum. He's taking French lessons. He spends time at the National Archives in Washington, D.C., where he's researching a book he wants to write, because half his family fought on the South in the Civil War and half on the North. He can do these things because two years before he retired, the company paid a professional consultancy to help him prepare for a new stage in his life. He's still advancing, and his employer retains his best value even after he's "retired."

Advancing your best people means separating the highest potential employees— your A-level players—and giving them special training, a place in succession planning, and goals and rewards that will stretch them. Not everybody wants the additional rewards and stresses of growth, but in your own mission to

MY POV

"You don't have to be big. I like a company that's 30 or 40 people. There is no question [as research Saatchi & Saatchi has done for 15 years bears out] that the more you feel like a family, the more successful you are over the long haul. Family's a metaphor, obviously, but while you're doing business, you can feel like a family in terms of trust, sacrifice, health, standing for each other, sharing doings, sharing sayings, sharing belongings, which is what families do. You will probably perform better over the long haul. But the more you can create a family environment, it seems to us, the more successful you will be."

—Kevin Roberts, CEO, Saatchi & Saatchi

build a great workplace, you have to focus extra resources on the people who will deliver greater value.

Many of the best employees will stay longer than you thought as long as they think that they are growing in their careers or they are building up their skill sets. They are advancing their knowledge and extending their current skill set.

The ultimate retention factor is an employee's engagement, and the employer brands we admire—Nike, Nordstrom, Google, and a hundred smaller firms—work because their people are living the brand promise. Those organizations hire the right people, for the right reasons, and then treat them right. There are no surprises except good ones.

Every spring, the Great Place to Work Institute, the Society for Human Resource Management, several magazines, and a number of local business journals publish lists of the best places to work. It takes a lot of commitment to get on those lists. While you're building an employment brand to feature yourself as a great place to work, you can take steps to become a great place to stay, and give your poised employees, at the moment they have a choice, the right reasons to choose you.

Review

- Calculate the true cost of turnover, including lost value from highly skilled employees.
- Survey both poised and loyalist employees confidentially, to find out the causes of turnover and reasons that good employees stay.
- Build a retention practice belonging to managers first, and hold them accountable.
- Create an onboarding program to build engagement in the critical early days for each employee.
- Build a long-term, individually responsive and flexible program to advance your keepers. It's how you'll keep them.

Chapter 10

Finding Keepers Globally

S pin a globe and put your finger down on the next hot country for recruiting. Everyone wants a piece of the globalized, capitalized, interconnected dream. Everyone's learning English, everyone's setting up call centers. Everyone's competing for the next Toyota assembly plant: China, India, Brazil, Romania, Turkey, Ireland, Kenya, Hungary, Malaysia. Every country with universities, a stable political environment, and bandwidth is becoming a source of skilled workers—and a competitor for skills.

The worldwide competition for talent affects more than multinational corporations. Medium and even smaller businesses in America compete for the best abroad, and overseas outsourcing becomes just one more component in a decentralized business structure. Need an accountant to handle your taxes? He might live in Prague. Doing a deal in Denver? Your due diligence team might use legal help that originates overseas. It all compounds the talent puzzle, tempting employers with the promise of more skilled workers, but requiring new methods to hire and hold them.

Candidates and employees from different cultures will experience your employment brand differently, and your understanding of the cultural difference must guide your methods and messages around finding keepers in any part of the world. We'll use two examples, China and India, throughout this chapter to illustrate ways in which understanding the cultural context around hiring and holding talent guides specific actions.

One key understanding is that the talented individual no longer stops her job search at the water's edge. North America is still a prime destination for talent worldwide . . . but so are Australia, the European Union (E.U.), the Pacific Rim, and South America, as well as parts of the Middle East and the former Soviet Republics. Younger generations of skilled workers—the future of your workforce—cross borders more easily than their parents did, either within their employers' multinational offices or when they switch jobs.

The worldwide nature of the talent shortage is putting a strain on recruiting just about everywhere. According to a 2007 Manpower survey, 60 percent of Pacific Rim employers and 40 percent of European Union employers report difficulty in filling positions. China's generation-long one-child policy is causing shortages of experienced middle management. In 2007, 61 percent of Australian companies reported difficulty filling positions with available talent; 40 percent of French companies said likewise and an incredible 93 percent of companies in Costa Rica reported that they had difficulty filling positions.[1] The legal situation varies among nations, as does each economy's need for foreign talent; but for any business attempting to bring foreign talent into its home country, the problem remains: there isn't enough talent to go around, and everyone is competing for it.

Other complications include the willingness of governments to provide work visas, legal and regulatory restrictions, and intercompany issues of fairness, talent development, and risk. To cite just one example, the computer maker Dell relocated its high-level business support group from the United

States to India in 2003. Customers complained so bitterly about the falloff in quality that Dell rerelocated that service back to the United States. One reason cited for the problems: the difficulty of finding enough top-notch support people in India.[2]

In this welter of changes, finding keepers in new locations is complex, if full of potential. Every country, region, and culture presents opportunities to connect with talent, and Internet technologies make the connection efficient. There is scale involved: a company with 20 employees isn't likely to open an office in Moldova next year, but it might have to cast its net a little farther than Main Street to find all the right talent. In an increasingly globalized business environment, talent appears beyond the borders of your country and perhaps of your imagination.

Bringing Talent In

If you're counting on getting the highly skilled talent you need just by trolling international waters, count again. Companies worldwide often look overseas to bring talent in. In the United States the H1-B visa is issued to highly skilled foreign workers. Businesses must sponsor individuals and apply to the U.S. government in April for visas issued in the following year. Congress sets an annual limit to the number of visas. In April 2007, when Congress set a limit of 65,000 visas, the government announced that it had received 150,000 applications on the first day. Other programs—for example, the programs for temporary or seasonal workers in fields such as health care, agriculture, and construction—add a small number of workers. In the United States and throughout the world, immigration is a hot political topic, and the uncertainty surrounding the issue makes planning difficult at best. Suffice it to say, if you are looking to acquire talent that requires elaborate legal work with the government, keep it to a manageable level.

Kent Kirch, the head of global recruiting at professional services leader Deloitte, observes: "People want [overseas recruiting] to be the entire solution to their shortage of talent. And I usually tell them, don't plan on more than 10 percent of your solution coming from recruiting abroad."

We agree with Kent's estimate at the moment, especially when we factor in the effects of visa issues, the cost of applying, the time it takes to recruit long distance, and your own learning curve.

The visa programs are only part of the story.

If you keep a realistic view today of the potential contribution that overseas recruiting can make to your workforce, however, you will see that learning how to bring in talent from overseas, even at a small scale, prepares you for more to come.

Workers of all skill levels are drawn to the United States, the European Union, the Pacific Rim, and developed countries throughout the world. A new fluidity is evident among young and accomplished professionals. Their ties are less binding to one company and to one country. Expatriates can be found everywhere. Thanks to the Internet, these skilled designers, accountants, engineers, and business professionals can find you easily—and vice versa.

The two questions that matter to workers you would like to hire from other countries are "do I wish to relocate to the employer's area?" and "what opportunity does the company offer?" Your employment brand message to them must address both of these topics.

You can't change the weather in Vancouver, but you can craft a message about life there that will attract people who love the outdoors. You can't make Tokyo less congested but you can promote its world-class cultural attractions in art, music, fashion, and entertainment. How do you attract someone from a European capital to live in Santiago? Talk about schools, the cost of living, and kids growing up in a safe and open-minded community.

Your core employer brand doesn't alter overseas. Although the ability to work in different countries presents many opportunities, your workplace cultures throughout the world need to attract the people who will fit your values and mission.

A well-constructed Web site can show anyone, anywhere what it's like to work in your organization, and it should, but don't expect it to attract talented people on its own. Get your message out to local resources in countries where you would like to recruit. Link your job descriptions and your employer branding to Web sites, organizations, and venues where international-minded workers gather, such as career sites, professional association sites, and the other places described in Chapters 6 and 7. Tailor your messages to their particular preferences. For example, you might offer the opportunity to work in several offices both in your home country or abroad, effectively incorporating travel into the job description.

> *You can't make Tokyo less congested but you can promote its world-class cultural attractions in art, music, fashion, and entertainment.*

This undertaking is hard to do without a real knowledge of local mores, popular culture, and traditions, and for this know-how you probably need a partner with local experience. Successful international advertisers get this point and translate brand messages according to local cultures and even local senses of humor. At Monster, we tailor our message to local markets in the advertising we do in the two dozen or so countries we serve—we notice that what's funny in one country isn't necessarily funny in another.

Recruiting for Offices Overseas

Companies and organizations—of every size—that operate internationally often expand by buying businesses similar to theirs overseas, and those firms will have recruiting staff in place. This is the fastest way to get local recruiting know-how, but it still requires integration with the practices and business culture of the parent company.

Internationally, hiring managers and recruiters are called upon to overcome differences more profound than in other disciplines. If a company decides to manufacture a widget in another country, the operations people pretty much know how to build that widget. If it wants to hire and manage talent in another country, it has to deal with different company-employee relationships, candidate expectations, cultures, laws, and values.

MY POV

"Internationally, executives are very interested in emerging opportunities in Russia, China, and India, and new innovation economies in the European Union. They see a talent gold rush, where about 50 percent of executives have expressed a willingness to work overseas, at least for a while. To compete in the global marketplace for talent, you will soon have to sell your country or region as a location as much as the company you work for and the jobs you have available. This will require that global recruiting teams think even more like marketers than ever before and learn how to position their own cultures and countries against others."

—*David Lefko, recruiting consultant*

With that in mind, we suggest that the focus of recruiting leaders should be preserving the principles of employment branding through the setup and execution of a recruiting strategy overseas. Your employer brand has to adjust within a multinational environment; your vision and your values can be replicated around the world. Our experience is that people can share company mission, vision, and values whether they are in Baltimore, Bangalore, Beijing, or Budapest.

The cultural context of work, however, might be completely different in one country versus another. The following are three examples.

Today in India, turnover is rampant and salaries are going up 15 to 25 percent a year. People move around a lot. It's unrealistic to hire people based on whether or not they want to make a career at your company. You can't attract the best talent in India today with a promise of job security, because it's irrelevant. More important today is what pay you offer and what opportunities you have for advancement. This situation might change as the gap between Western and Indian salaries narrows, but for the moment it's the message that conforms to the business culture.

In China, the theme of "work hard, play hard" is not acceptable because people work hard, period. The sales reps we know arrive in the morning, sing the company song, and get right to work. At noon they take a lunch break, at 12:30 they turn off the lights, unroll mats from under their desks, and take a 30-minute nap. Then they work until eight or nine at night.

Many of the people who work with Monster in China today are the first in their family to aspire to own an automobile or a piece of property some day, and living "the good life" has a different material meaning from its image elsewhere. If you or your parents were born in a far province, where you didn't have running water, indoor plumbing, or electricity, much less a phone or TV, what's a better life? Today, the good life is not a big house in the suburbs—it's the chance to be self-sufficient, maybe get a phone, get a car, and have more than one change of clothes for work.

There are obviously lots of smart, talented people in China. That country is experiencing talent shortages of its own. There's a cultural sense, however, that this situation is all new. There's a consensus that getting a good job and working hard leads to a good life. You don't hear a lot of dialogue that people in Western countries engage in about increasing your satisfaction or fulfillment through work and earning a lot more leisure time.

That's not a subtle difference.

For the third example, try to apply the American cliché—"we live to work"—to Europe. Monster has a technical development center in Prague, and it's attracted a lot of great talent from Eastern Europe, including people with Ph.D.'s from Russia and Ukraine. They grew up in a European culture that, while it works hard, savors the good things in life too. If Americans live to work, Europeans work to live. They're hugely productive, but on Friday night, they go home or out with friends and socialize. Whereas in the United States managers take work home on Friday and all weekend they're e-mailing each other. You don't see that much in Europe.

Imagine approaching skilled workers in Europe with the same recruiting message that you would use in China or India! Obviously you have to understand the different cultures to approach people appropriately in the different situations. Employers have to be careful that their employment brand adjusts to such cultural norms. Your vision, mission, and values remain the same; the core attributes of your employment brand stay in place. The differences are found in the tangible and intangible benefits you offer.

You focus different tangible benefits based on prevailing economic conditions. To cite an obvious difference: if everyone in the country gets national health care insurance, offering a great health plan won't attract or retain people the way it does in the United States. In China, training is highly valued, as is respect from your manager, while current conditions in India promote money as the tangible benefit that outweighs others by a large margin.

Recruiting in China

China is producing a lot of graduates, but not the right type, and this outcome causes shortages. While there is an oversupply of some young workers, and starting salaries have eased for five years, there are shortages of experienced, capable managers. Wages for them are rising.

Even at the top 100 universities in China, most learning is academic memorization. There's little development of skills like problem solving, communication, teamwork, project management, and similar skills that are taught in Western colleges. As a result, even top graduates have to learn the business methods to get the job done, ask for help, resolve conflicts, and manage complex or changing projects. There's been a big increase in technical schools but they are highly specialized, graduating electrical engineers or auto engineers. These skilled workers are making more money than their business counterparts.

cont'd on page 183

Cont'd from page 182

In the early decades of its opening up, Chinese business was dominated by state- and government-owned enterprises with different methods, values, and priorities than classic capitalist businesses. Today, you'll see that managers in China's financial services sector are mostly from Taiwan, Singapore, and Hong Kong. Until China's education system changes and native Chinese managers get enough experience, businesses working in China will suffer shortages of key people.

Here's my advice to recruiters working in China:

1. Do not believe that operating in China means that there will be a large, cheap labor supply. Even where that situation is true, at the entry level or in manufacturing jobs, there are key shortages of experience.

2. Understand that everyone is looking for talent. Small and medium-size businesses compete with giant multinational corporations as well as native Chinese companies, state-owned industries, and government, and they'll compete on price as well as prestige.

3. Prestige still matters. I often hear a candidate declare, "I want to work in a five-star office building not a four-star office building."

4. Geographic differences are dramatic in terms of labor cost, business methods, business policy, and available talent. Shanghai and Beijing elites are looking for different intangibles as well as tangible rewards.

5. Local jurisdictions have more clout than in the West. China has thousands of high-tech industrial parks, and they vary widely in business conditions. You might get a 5 percent tax break for opening a plant in X location, and 14 percent in location Y, just 100 kilometers away ... but you can't attract talent to location Y.

6. Local labor traditions are surprisingly strong. We say that everyone in Fujian, in the south, goes elsewhere to work. In fact, when I worked for Wal-Mart in China, almost all of its cashiers in Fujian

cont'd on page 184

Cont'd from page 183

were from other regions, and Fugianese were famously the ethnic Chinese entrepreneurs in Malaysia, Indonesia, the Philippines, and the West. In the north, people are much more likely to stay close to home. Traditions still effect work patterns more in China than elsewhere. Learn the cultural work conditions where you plan to do business.

—Jim Yang, Monster account manager, China

Staffing an office overseas requires a good understanding of the cultural preference for how tangible benefits are structured as well.

You'll find a clear example in sales compensation: For example, in the United States a common base salary-to-commission ratio is 40/60 whereas in Europe it is more like 70/30. Americans will accept a lower guaranteed salary in exchange for a higher upside potential, but in Europe the compensation isn't as crucial as security and predictability. The setup that drives the entire sales force in the United States doesn't work as well in Europe, and vice versa. And yet the mission, the vision, the opportunity to win . . . all the things that sales pros in the United States love, the Europeans love too. They're passionate about succeeding, about winning; but the compensation structure has to reflect a different feeling about risk.

Colloquy: Going Global

How do you bring intangible benefits to workplaces globally? When just managing a single office is hard enough, what practices work when three, five, or fifty offices have to think globally but recruit locally?

We asked Kent Kirch, global director of recruiting at professional services firm Deloitte, to discuss these and other global implementation questions. What follows is a colloquy on global hiring from the front lines:

Steve Pogorzelski: How do you adjust the intangible rewards in your employment brand overseas?

Kent Kirch: The big question is, how do you design or adapt your branding to match the local circumstances? We found that the mission, the vision, and the values have to be the same globally, so we've distilled down the essence of the brand, not just by country but even by groups within a country—like MBAs versus undergrads or experienced professionals versus entry-level employees, and there are different messages for those groups.

Anyone wanting to develop a global brand has to do some research. One, how are you currently perceived in the marketplace by the people you're looking to recruit? You might think you're one thing, but you're actually another in the eyes of your potential candidates. Two, what are people currently inside the organization experiencing? If you overpromise on the employment experience, you'll just cause turnover because people will come in and they'll be disappointed.

You learn that the things people are looking for in an employer can vary pretty significantly depending on what country you're in. That's been an eye-opener for me over the last year.

Steve: We found the same thing in our employee satisfaction surveys internally. In Europe, they're looking for an employer who emphasizes and has empathy with work-life balance, whereas in Asia Pacific it's how people are managed and the respect they get from their immediate superiors that's of far greater importance than work-life balance.

Kent: I would add that, in some of those developing countries, the opportunity to learn has been especially important, both from work and company-sponsored education.

Steve: How soon do you need boots on the ground when you're placing a group overseas?

Kent: Yesterday. All leaders want recruiting people in place as soon as possible, searching for talent. The first thing I hear in any country is that recruiters feel they've tapped out the marketplace in that location for talent. So they name a country or a group of countries or a region in the world where they think there's an excess of talent. They've all read these articles about China and India, and so they just assume talent's available and can easily be transported to wherever they need them. That's all over the world.

So the first question I have to ask is, "What haven't you done so far where you live? Recruiting across borders is going to be a lot more time-consuming and expensive than recruiting locally. Let's make sure you really are totally tapped out in your home country first. And then if it's obvious they are tapped out, then we start to have discussions about where the profiles that they're looking for might be located and available.

Kent: Right now, there's a lot of bidding going on for talent in China and India because so many companies are locating operations there for all the same reasons. It's just like the dot-com era in Silicon Valley—the marketplace heats up, everyone's bidding for the same skills and that generates a huge amount of turnover.

Steve: When we look at the Monster Employment Indexes internationally, it's clear that the acute skills shortages we have in occupational categories in the United States are very similar to the acute skill shortages you see in Europe. We're beginning to see them in India as well.

For us as a business, retention has come to the fore very quickly in the hiring cycle in Asia. We've started talking about long-term incentive compensation in India and China, but particularly in India. This might mean getting greater numbers of people involved there with our bonus programs than have been in the past. Then the recruiting conversation can be more about a candidate's contribution three to five years down the road, not necessarily whether he can make 10 percent more this year if he walks across the street.

Kent: I think public companies have a real advantage there in terms of ways they can address not only compensation on a longer-term basis but also a sense of ownership. If you're able to use stock ownership, for example, to increase an employee's financial stake in the company, there's a higher emotional investment as well.

Steve: So instead of offering a little bit more money, you change the game to offering the opportunity to advance, long-term incentive compensation, training, on-the-job learning, respect from your manager, and the chance to belong to a great company. That's employer branding.

Kent: What has been really interesting to watch over the last three to five years is Internet adoption and the ease of communicating. That has really helped us as a large organization with operations all over the world to try and at least have some alignment and consistency around how we go to market for recruitment. So it's actually much more consistent than one might expect.

Steve: We try not to impose a North American or Anglo-American approach to anything we do. But once you've found something that works in more than one location, it's generally going to work everywhere. Who are Deliotte's crucial company players between home and overseas?

Kent: It depends on the market. Our organization is different in that in most cases the business we have in any given country was born there on its own and later became part of Deloitte. Other companies have to find or import HR talent. That being said, there are some places where there is a very limited or maybe even almost nonexistent supply of HR and recruiting talent above a managerial level.

It's very, very difficult to find people who have any depth of experience in recruitment and HR in India and China. Particularly in China, where the market's only been open for a short period of time, there just isn't enough senior-level talent in many professions, including HR. But because of that, we've brought in talent from other places, not necessarily the United States, where we had that senior talent. Their mission is to go in there for two or three years, find someone with the right potential, groom them, coach them along and leave the business with an effective HR leader when they leave.

Steve: How do you get your best practices working for everyone globally?

Kent: We say, "Here's the best practice we know for a particular outcome. Now you have to either prove it or disprove it, based on the needs of your market, or better it." But at least we start with the best practice that was proven somewhere else. We do this whether it's an employee referral program that's been highly successful or a particular tool that's worked real well, or a selection methodology that works well. Then the challenge is to ask people to adapt to it, unless they have a business case for not doing it. Interestingly, the dynamic changes when a practice comes from somewhere in the world other than headquarters. People in other regions are actually pretty highly motivated to make it work for them.

Steve: We've had success in recruiting and other functions with a practice we call "Flatten the World Forums." We bring certain functions together on a global basis, typically not in the United States, and have the local groups share best practices, without those practices being dictated. It's less threatening, and certainly the innovation level goes up when that occurs. Most global talent supply problems have implications for managing the company, not just recruiting.

Kent: Deloitte has a Global Recruitment Council made up of 25 national recruiting leaders. The group looks for best practices around our organization. Typically we find something that's worked in one country but has to be adapted. A working group takes a proven concept—

a referral program, for example—and brings experience from multiple locations to it. That group creates a model program that is spread through the organization as a blueprint. That Council helps with the whole buy-in process globally.

Steve: Looking forward, how will a global shortage of skills play out?

Kent: The questions are: how many people will actually continue to work either full- or part-time after the traditional retirement age and what will immigration patterns look like? Talent retention will be the key to business survival. Attracting talent will always be important, but recruiting yourself out of the talent shortage alone will not be a sustainable strategy.

Just a few years ago, nobody really thought of India or China as a source of strong quality people. Now they are leading an international revolution in legal and accounting and IT and other professional work. Other countries, large and small, have bet their economic future on building a skilled workforce, and slowly, beginning with multinational companies but driving down to medium and smaller businesses, organizations are finding talent without borders.

People might not move as freely among countries as they might wish, but in an interdependent and networked world, that might not matter, because even where the movement of people is restricted, the movement of work, ideas, and service—in short, the movement of economic value—continues to accelerate. In the words of journalist Thomas L. Friedman, "They're not racing us to the bottom; they're racing us to the top."

Even on this global scale, what matters is the match. Your ability to advance your employment brand globally, and cast your recruiting net worldwide, is the key to bringing aboard these talented, borderless, and valuable employees.

Review

- The globalized talent market means that all developed economies face a similar pattern of shortages—only the details change.
- When you are planning for the near future, expect no more than 10 percent of your in-country workforce to come from overseas, and plan to expand operations where the talent lives.
- When working overseas, think globally in terms of recruiting methods and the employment brand.
- Think locally for applying the recruiting brand to outreach (for example, advertising). Build, buy, or partner for local knowledge quickly.
- People move quite freely among countries worldwide than most people realize; use cross-country migration to help staff overseas operations.

Chapter 11

Next Practices

Robert Crowder, now senior executive recruiter at Aetna, Inc., had to overcome a daunting challenge when he was director of diversity staffing at The Hartford Financial Services Group:

It's an insurance company with big growth prospects in diverse communities (African-American, Asian-American, Hispanic, and a wealth of others). We needed a diverse workforce to reach those prospects, but those candidates tend to be hip, young, and brand-conscious. How do you get them excited about a business with such a buttoned-down reputation? You bring them the right brand message.

We know our employees feel good about working there. We also know that personal interaction is the most effective advertising to diverse populations. So we engaged our employees with diverse professional organizations like the International Association of Black Actuaries or the National Association of Black Accountants or the Association of Latinos in Finance and Accounting. Our senior executives spoke at those meetings about the many reasons our employees feel good about the mission, work-life balance, and values [of the company]. They gave seminars on all kinds of jobs, and those professionals said, 'I didn't realize you could have that kind of job in the insurance business.'

The Engagement Cycle addresses the three current waves of change we described in Chapter 1. A little farther over the horizon are more waves of change: long-term trends in business, technology, and culture that offer new threats and new opportunities to hire and hold the best. The evolution of diversity recruiting, led by practitioners like Robert Crowder, is one of those.

The changing relationships among employers, candidates, and employees are driven by at least six trends combining technology, demographics, and culture; they are transparency, interactivity, mobility, diversity, flexibility, and community. Employers that embrace these trends will go beyond today's best practices and adopt the "next practices" that will be the most promising and progressive methods for finding keepers in the coming decade.

Some employers think that "sooner or later there will be a recession; the pendulum will swing back to me. Candidates will lose bargaining power, and I'll be back in the driver's seat." In effect, they are saying they can wait out a talent shortage without changing to adopt the practices we have put forward in this book.

We doubt they can wait it out. The trends driving next practices will change how candidates and poised workers behave even in recession. They increase the autonomy and value of the most talented keepers in the marketplace. Employers who learn next practices will see their potential pool of talent grow as the best candidates respond to their brands. Employers who believe that the Engagement Cycle ends at an economic slowdown will occupy the second tier of brands in the mind of poised candidates and employees.

Transparency

Imagine a marketplace saturated with information—the conversation and the engagement never stops among buyer, seller, and intermediaries that have something to say about both buyer and seller. It already exists at eBay and a thousand other shopping sites where buyers and sellers meet. The consumers are in control of where to buy, what to buy, and what information they get when they buy, and that is extending to the hiring process.

Candidates will find detailed narratives about employers online and will be able to judge the authenticity of employer brands. Beyond the star ratings for products you find today on sites like CNET.com, think of the thoughtful, lengthy collections of reviews you find on Amazon.com. Candidates will also judge the veracity of the reviews, depending on their source.

Right now candidates have access to job postings and company backgrounds, and a little bit of opinion (often unreliable) from message boards. Soon candidates will be able to get more information about what it's like to work in a company through videos or postings or aggregated content across the Web, so they can learn all of the good and the bad before they show up for interviews. Sources of information will be rated for their reliability and accuracy.

What will all this easy-to-get information mean for employers? It will mean that the reality of working for the company will be out there for all to see, which is great news for employers with strong workplace experiences and scary news for businesses that treat people like "assets." The recruiting function will put less emphasis on direct selling and more on managing the employer brand, channels of communication, and long-term relationships with prospective candidates. There will be much more emphasis on consciously crafting an employer brand message that is authentic to the employer brand experience, because those who don't create the experience themselves will be stuck with whatever the marketplace says about them.

Currently, a few recruiting software systems inform a candidate of their status during the recruiting process, and this capability answers the highly charged problem of applications falling into a black hole. As recruiters at Johnson & Johnson learned, candidates respect feedback, even when the news is disappointing. Candidates might receive a tracking number and regular e-mail updates on the progress of their candidacy, similar to the way a package is tracked today by UPS and FedEx. If you're familiar with these companies' order status system, imagine a candidate logging into your Web site, post-application, and receiving a "where's my résumé?" update. (Internally, this kind of tracking system serves to move candidates through the funnel as well—communicating interview status and feedback to all concerned while guarding confidential information.)

Employers will know more about candidates from a variety of sources. Employers will be able to search more effectively to get the backgrounds of people, not only from a legal standpoint but also in terms of what those people have accomplished at work. Successful candidates will have rich narratives of work accomplishments, perhaps from intermediaries; perhaps on their own in the form of ever-more-sophisticated Web sites. You see an early form of this in the "recommendations" on LinkedIn.com

> *The recruiting function will put less emphasis on direct selling and more on managing the employer brand, channels of communication, and long-term relationships.*

Employers will make job matches in ways that reflect more subtle criteria. For example, you might be able to take a résumé of somebody who's leaving, stick it into the system, and get perfect matches for 10 candidates to replace the departing employee. Even after 12 years of search development, recruiters often still sift through a lot of information; search technology is going to be a lot more powerful and subtle in 10 years, and we'll be referring not to résumé search but to candidate search, as software compiles a portfolio of information about each candidate drawn from public and private databases of information that candidates have chosen to share.

Interactivity

The Engagement Cycle is already interactive, because it represents an ongoing, changing relationship, and inputs from both sides affect the outcome. Interactivity is becoming more intense in both employer branding work and in candidate approaches.

"Entercruitment," the packaging of an employer brand message in an entertaining media experience, attracts and educates candidates while reinforcing the brand. Branches of the military have done impressive work in this area with their online recruiting sites, delivering recruiting messages and answering questions in virtual worlds. They have adapted video and gaming technologies expertly targeted to the young audience they seek. On the U.S. Army's recruiting site, an online avatar answers questions. The U.S. Marine Corps site, in contrast, has deconstructed its information in such a way that prospective recruits experience the corps' messages in the order they choose: animated images invite the prospective recruit to learn more about Marine life, history, training, and mission. Sound effects enhance the images. While the design is contemporary, the Marine's branding message remains strongly traditional, and the site is saturated with the language of Marine values. The experience is more than browsing—it's a self-guided tour through which the visitor finds his or her own route, immersed in a consistent branding message.

"Entercruitment" extends off-line as well. Today, the U.S. National Guard broadcasts its message in a 10-minute infomercial shown in movie theaters, and its tone is much closer to a documentary film than a hard sell appeal to join the guard.

Employer-created assessment is an entire world of interactivity, today's assessment testing is just the beginning. Candidates will be asked (or required) to validate their status with standardized assessment testing across key occupation categories. An employer will be able to understand a candidate's competencies and benchmark him against other candidates. Ultimately, this capability creates a type of human capital exchange in which employers choose which competencies are most meaningful to them. They can then focus on intangible, cultural, and personal matches to get the best fit.

Assessment of individuals will extend beyond traditional competencies to abilities such as problem solving and communication. Today, some employers feature problem-solving tests and even advanced case study problems on their recruitment sites, ranking responses and even delivering immediate feedback to the candidate. Soon, organizations will conduct interactive "auditions" in which candidates are invited to create solutions to existing problems, exploit current opportunities, and even propose new products. This is an extension of the most advanced interviewing techniques, so in a sense, interactivity is bringing a richer "job interview" to both sides earlier in the Engagement Cycle.

Mobility

Think of mobility in two ways, the mobility of information and the mobility of talent, because they go hand-in-hand.

We are well down the technological path of mobile information. Poised candidates will receive messages about potential work opportunities anytime and anywhere, just as they receive stock market alerts on their cell phones now. In China, cell phones outnumber personal computers four to one and are the obvious platform for sending job alerts as well as employment branding messages. For example, Monster's Jim Yang mentions that prestigious work locations are a big selling point; imagine sending a video clip of your beautiful new offices in Shanghai to the phones of thousands of candidates you've identified as potential employees, with an invitation to browse available jobs.

Mobile technology will increasingly allow employers to target brand messages to candidates by geographic, demographic, or psychographic data. As mobile adoption increases, there will be the opportunity for recruiters to find workers quickly based on the geolocating capabilities in workers' phones. For example, will you need 15 laborers next Tuesday at a job site near downtown? Tools will enable you to locate and reach out to candidates near the site. Furthermore, employers will be able to screen and filter candidates in real time using interactive mobile applications. If you want to reach sales representatives with five years' experience and a five-star productivity rating, who have identified themselves as poised, within 20 miles of Chicago's Loop, and with experience in selling services, hit the Send key. You'll be able to send a text message or video, whichever one a rep prefers.

As more recruiters use mobile devices directly, recruiting in field locations will become easier as well. Mobile tools are being developed to help recruiters assess candidates quickly, such as employment histories and candidate information via a mobile phone. We've seen some exciting start-up companies which are developing technologies like this focused on the HR community.

Mobile social networking will also evolve to help recruiters and candidates find one another. Companies like Jaiku, MobiLuck, and Enpresence are developing platforms that can be used by recruiters and candidates to let you know when someone in your network is nearby.

Shorter hiring cycles will result from rich information flowing between employer and candidate more or less continuously, and candidates will come to expect a quicker process. This presents an opportunity for smaller and less bureaucratic organizations that can move from attraction to job offer in a day or two. That kind of speed is possible when much is already known about candidates in advance and the employer is nimble enough to act quickly. The employer that can get to three finalists rapidly will benefit both internally, with a quicker ramp-up to productivity, and externally, by moving candidates toward quicker decision making. (Incidentally, this quick vetting might also become a way for employers to head off the possibility of some candidates receiving multiple offers or sandbagging their current employers for a better deal.)

In this context, "hiring cycle" comes to mean the brief period when employer and candidate are actively discussing a specific position. It becomes a smaller portion of the Engagement Cycle—a few days in a career-long relationship.

Finally, the trend toward personal mobility, especially in younger workers, will continue to make work less dependent on everyone assembling in a certain time at a certain place. This will increase both nontraditional work arrangements (see the section on "Flexibility" later in this chapter) and the global hiring trends seen in Chapter 10. There are significant differences in personal mobility among national populations. A 2005 McKinsey & Co. study found, for example, that only 6 percent of Russians outside of the cosmopolitan hubs of Moscow and St. Petersburg were willing to relocate for work. In China, more workers expressed a willingness to relocate, but the demand for talent there is so strong that few felt the need to leave China strictly to find better employment.[1]

Communications technology feeds the trend toward mobility, and also makes working abroad, working from home, or working across the country more feasible for employees and the employers who can adjust their workplace methods to suit the mobile employee.

Diversity

"New consumer segments have always represented an opportunity to get new customers and increase profits," says Monster's Chief Diversity Officer Steve Pemberton. "Today there are more emerging consumer and business segments than ever, and this is accelerating. People of different backgrounds, cultures, and preferences are acquiring greater purchasing power. The makeup of the workforce, especially younger people who represent the future of the workforce, is more racially, ethnically, and culturally diverse than ever."

Steve continues: "The drivers of diversity recruiting have changed, and the conversation has moved from social activism and compliance—do the right thing and don't get sued—to opening new markets and improving bottom lines. Managers who embrace diversity hiring from this point of view are on the verge of delivering much more value to their business."

You need a more diverse workforce to develop products that customers want and reach them on their terms. When the drivers of diversity change to more traditional business concerns, the questions of diversity recruiting change from *whether* (yes) and *when* (yesterday) to *how*.

As Robert Crowder's story at the beginning of this chapter demonstrates, diversity recruiting starts with understanding the audience you want to attract, and bringing your employer brand message to that audience early in the Engagement Cycle. Notice that he did not change the employer branding of The Hartford. Rather, he adapted a core message of the brand ("people feel good about working here") to the audience, and then went directly to the candidates he wanted to attract.

Monster's research[2] on diverse candidates in the United States finds several themes through which you can customize your recruiting messages:

Next Practices **199**

Compensation

Salary remains a dominant factor for candidates regardless of age, gender, or ethnicity, and so an employer must offer competitive salary and benefits packages just to get to the starting line. Salary is not, however, the only input that people use when making job decisions, and while more money might bring someone in the door, it often will not keep that person in the company.

Diverse candidates cite the same top reasons for leaving or staying with their current employers. Across all groups, difficult relationships and poor communication push people out: 29 percent of workers consider leaving because of conflicts with their boss or coworkers, and 34 percent consider leaving a job because they feel their work is not appreciated (22 percent in Monster's surveys actually left for this reason).

After those basic commonalities among all audiences, there are distinct preferences on which you can customize your message.

The Very Existence of a More Diverse Workforce Is Itself an Attraction to Many Candidates

Of the skilled workers Monster surveyed, 77 percent of African Americans, 70 percent of Asian Americans, and 65 percent of Hispanics stated that it is very important that the employer they are considering already have a diverse workforce. (Additionally, 46 percent of Caucasian employees feel that when considering job opportunities, it is very important that the company already has a diverse workforce.)

Opportunities for Training, Growth, and Career Progression Are Stronger Motivating Factors for Ethnically Diverse Job Seekers Than for Their Caucasian Counterparts

Seventy-six percent of minority workers consider opportunities for continued training and learning to be important when evaluating a new position, versus

64 percent of Caucasians. Eighty percent of African Americans and 77 percent of Hispanics rate opportunities to move up in the company as "important" versus only 63 percent of Caucasians.

Diverse Populations Look to Organizations to Demonstrate Their Commitment to Workplace Diversity

In Monster's studies, 85 percent of diverse employees agree that it is important to see people like themselves in positions of leadership.

African Americans, Asian Americans, and Hispanics all state that they look for information on a company's diversity policies as part of a job search. As Steve Pemberton of Monster advises, "Good intentions are fine, but you'd better be able to discuss policy issues like career pathing, succession planning, and support for professional education in detail when you recruit these audiences."

Men Focus More Heavily on Compensation and Career Growth While Women Place a Higher Value on Work-Life Balance

Men are more likely than women to rank salary as the single most important deal maker (45 percent versus 38 percent). A long commute, an inconvenient work location, and lack of flexibility in work hours are more frequently deal breakers for women than for men. Recruiters should not discount work-life issues when talking to men; it is an important factor to many male candidates, but they tend to focus on it only *after* entering a new workplace, whereas women currently examine work-life issues *during* the recruiting process.

Older Employees Place Greater Weight on Benefits and Retirement Plans

Sixty-seven percent of the 50+ segment considers a better pension or retirement plan a significant deal maker, whereas only 45 percent of 18- to 34-year-olds feel the same way. Fifty-six percent of young employees (ages 18 to 34) say they feel bored by their jobs, versus 33 percent of employees ages 50+.

Searching for more diverse résumés in databases or across the Web is no different from other searches: you have to discover what particular data different candidates might list on their résumés. Career sites allow candidates to look for jobs under "Diversity and Inclusion" criteria.

John Rice is founder and CEO of Management Leadership for Tomorrow (MLT), a national nonprofit that is addressing the underrepresentation of African Americans, Hispanics, and Native Americans in senior leadership positions. He describes how leading companies have developed relationship-based diversity recruiting:

> The folks who are winning are investing more deeply in the pipeline earlier and personalizing their process. They're moving from a short-term transactional model to a longer-term engagement, education, and preparation model.
>
> They identify candidates as early as their junior year in college, or their first year in business school, and then give them a roadmap for success: 'here's the employer brand; here's how to prepare for a career at our firm.' They keep in touch, and continue to expose the candidates to various opportunities and people, and that creates a broader window to tell their story and to identify the folks who can be the best fit for them. They're proactively building the qualifications of the talent pool while they recruit.
>
> Citigroup is a good example. They go to MBA programs where they've found strong talent in the past. When they identify diverse candidates through MLT or other sources, they'll reach out and engage those students with some of their younger line managers. Those younger managers follow up with regular contact, whether that's via e-mail or a phone call or a visit. The candidates relate to those younger managers, who are maybe two or three years out of school.

At the same time, Citigroup's most senior minority executives will engage promising candidates as they move further down the process. They happen to have executives who really care about this and want to be engaged. Candidates have some idea what15 minutes of these senior executives' time is worth, and that sends a strong message that Citigroup is serous about diversity and serious about them.

So it's a two-part branding and relationship strategy: The candidate can look up to the senior executive and identify with the younger manager. The senior executive embodies an employer brand, and the younger manager validates that brand.

The new movement of diversity in the workplace is not accompanied with a blare of trumpets. It's taking place quietly, as more recruiters and hiring managers understand why this is a business imperative. For any employer, large or small, facing a shortage of skilled workers and looking for new customers, diversity hiring programs are strategic.

Flexibility

Like mobility and interactivity, flexibility is a business and social trend affecting employers and talented workers simultaneously. Flexibility is the successful response to a rapidly changing competitive climate. (We should add that we mean flexibility in strategy and tactics; mission, values, and the organization's identity should be slower to change, if they change at all.)

The "free-agent" candidate embodies this flexibility in his career with different work arrangements through the years, growing and changing expertise, and a portfolio career of experiences and accomplishments versus up-the-ladder progression.

The new organization embodies flexibility in its execution of strategy, with flexible deployment of talent resources, decentralization of work groups, and a changing mix of full-time, part-time, contact, and temporary arrangements in its workforce.

For the purposes of finding keepers, flexibility is largely about work arrangements; what follows is an overview of trends we see accelerating.

Contract, Temporary, and Part-Time Workers

Every autumn, IBM's employees sign up for their next year's benefits. They have a wide range of options and lots of questions for the people in human resources. For about six weeks, the toll-free benefits line lights up with inquiries. Then, when everybody's signed up, the line goes quiet. IBM copes with the surge in benefits questions by adding temporary workers to its phone lines—but not just any temps. Working through staffing agency Veritude, IBM hires ex-IBM *employees* at a call center in North Carolina to explain the benefits and get people signed up. The ex-employees are mostly retirees who aren't ready to stop work entirely. Says Linda Stewart, who set up the program for Veritude: "It just happens to be a group of people that is looking for a balance between their work and their life. Because they understand the IBM culture so well, they speak the language of the current employees, know the options, and know their concerns." When the sign-up period is over, the current employees have had a good experience (compare it to the last time you tried to figure out your new benefits) and the temporary workers, their earnings pocketed, go back to a temporary retirement.

The skilled people you need aren't all working full time anymore, and you might not need them 50 weeks a year. Just as business is becoming more fragmented, with project work and seasonal hiring growing, more and more of the skilled workforce is stepping away from the old 9-to-5 arrangement. Highly qualified people are taking greater control of their work schedules, either by working part time (especially the boomers as they near retirement) or in contract arrangements. Increasingly, this is where you'll find the right combination of skills and schedule.

"The issues around flexibility are going to become more intense. . . . Can your people work remotely, can they work part-time, can they work on a project basis, can they work seasonally?" asks Kent Kirch of Deloitte. "Most employers will have to go there in order to keep the talent they want . . . or attract it in the first place."

These are among the most consumer-minded skilled workers, and they don't place all bets on a single employer. Progressive managers have learned that in less than a generation, the "temporary worker" population has grown beyond the seasonal sales clerk to include some of the most experienced and talented workers in the market, a group with some very specific requirements beyond pay. They take responsibility for managing their careers. They are highly alert to employer reputation. They are more sensitive to issues like getting paid in a timely manner. The most talented among them see an employer's willingness to engage them on their terms as a big plus in favor of that employer. The recruiter and managers who can attract and acquire this group on its terms will tap a powerful reservoir of skills at a time their competitors might not even see that reservoir.

Erin Bloom, director of marketing for talent at staffing firm Aquent Professional Services, gives an example of today's highly skilled temporary worker:

> We practice what we preach about using freelancers. One freelancer saved us last summer when we were redesigning the Aquent Web site. Our design agency was not meeting our deadlines and the Aquent freelancer was able to step up and start turning work around for us very quickly. Now he is building Web sites for several of our clients in Philadelphia, and he has become a shining example of Aquent talent. We recognize good talent, especially people who can come through for us in a bind, and we try hard to keep them happy.

Understand that you can earn the loyalty of contract or part-time employees by cultivating a strong working relationship and recognizing their talents. Can your organization give a leadership role to a part-timer? Can your best network operations analyst work 20-hour weeks for a year so she has time to train for her next triathlon? If not, you might be deciding that hiring the second-best is better than becoming more flexible.

This is a structural change. You have to attract and acquire this population differently. You have to compensate them differently, train them differently, manage them differently—and you have to get all those pieces of your organization working together to make it successful. If your training program runs for six weeks from nine to five, without exceptions, you're not going to get those people working for you.

The employer brand has to be clear on this issue. For example, a company culture that rewards its hardest-driving people with promotions, money, and prestige based on their long hours and high levels of achievement (think Wall Street, start-ups, and law firms) should be clear that work-life balance comes at a price. That company will attract candidates with a certain lifestyle, and discourage others from joining—perhaps an acceptable trade-off when there are an unlimited number of workaholics coming out of graduate school but not necessarily a path to greatness over the long term.

Some firms, such as consulting leader Ernst & Young, are creating a third way on issues of work-life balance, offering a balanced lifestyle with high reward to as an alternative to the take-it-or-leave-it formulas. Ernst & Young's "Working Moms Network" encourages women and men who strive for greater work-family balance to form a community, to network with one another, and to represent this new wave of workers as company culture develops.

Attracting these candidates is actually not very difficult, because your ability to manage around their needs is a strong selling point. Your employer brand should feature that. You can state in advertising that you offer flexible schedules. Your Web site can feature testimonials from employees with nontraditional arrangements, and your recruiting staff can be conversant with part-time work options. Since people in this population can be somewhat reticent to bring the issue forward at once, bring it up yourself in all your networking and referral efforts. Make the fact that you are actively looking for these people a reason for them to select you over your competition.

Finding these folks is easier than changing to accommodate them. Résumé databases allow you to search for part-time and contract workers, and adding these terms to a Web résumé search is easy. Those who maintain personal Web sites are usually clear about their status.

Implications for the Staffing Industry

No business is more profoundly affected by this growing phenomenon of workplace flexibility than the staffing industry. (We define "staffing firms" here as those recruiters who place people in temporary or contract assignments in other companies. The people are employees of the staffing firms, who are paid by the client companies for their services.) If you work in this business, you are both victim and beneficiary of the talent squeeze, says John Hennessy, Monster's senior vice president of Staffing.

John supplies this analysis based on his years working with staffing companies:

The challenge faced by staffing firms is exactly the skilled worker shortage we've discussed, which is compounded by the fact that a staffing company's "product" is primarily skilled workers! The people you must bring to your customer are just as much part of the talent shortage as the full-time work-force. There are 2.9 million people working in temporary staffing jobs today, and most of them have the choice to register with several staffing agencies and work with whomever places them. They can choose to accept assignments or reject them. You need them, and the best of them are more independent and demanding than ever.

The employer customer wants a high-quality candidate. Having an important role vacant for an extended period of time can destroy a project and cost real money, so you're expected to move fast. Your customer is often bidding the job out to several firms, and once a job is filled, it's gone.

Your great opportunity is to become the single solution to both the con-tract worker's desire for an arrangement other than full time, single-employer status, and the employer's lack of resources in recruiting the right people in the middle of a skills shortage. The staffing firms have the opportunity to become classic "arms merchants," serving both sides of the talent equation.

John explains that many staffing firms fail to exploit this enviable position fully because they fall into a transactional trap: "Many staffing companies have a perspective that recruiters should spend 100 percent of their time filling the job orders, and use spare time to fill their pipeline with new talent. The ones who are really successful, however, dedicate at least 30 percent of recruiter time to discovering additional candidates and building rapport with the employees they have placed. Their recruiters network in professional associations, user groups and college placement offices. They attract talent by getting involved in the community. They use job boards, they check in with talent they haven't talked to in a few months. They invest their own time and energy in marketing themselves and branding their company to the talent that they need to supply their customers with temporary workers."

As specialists, staffing firms need to demonstrate progressive methods of finding and matching skilled people and jobs. (Otherwise, what value do they add?) Sometimes the winning methods are simple—we know a staffing firm that noticed that job seeker traffic to career Web sites accelerates on Sunday night and peaks on Monday. The firm put a group of recruiters on the job Sunday afternoon. The recruiters talked to potential talent at exactly the moment gloomy thoughts about "Blue Monday" made them open to a recruiter's pitch.

In order to exploit this opportunity, you need to apply all the principles of marketing and branding we've discussed to make your firm's employer brand compelling to candidates. When candidates feel that they are part of your organization, then you have a strong service to sell to your employer customers. You can expand the relationship from a transactional, fill-this-job-requisition-NOW basis to a strategic, consultative, long-term basis.

Erin Bloom tells how this consultative approach benefits both sides:

We've been staffing people within marketing departments for 20 years. We study how great marketing organizations work, and we have a consulting group that teaches marketing organizations how they can function more effectively.

For example, a client may call us and say, "I need a graphic designer right away." After some conversations, we might determine that they actually need a production artist, which is less expensive than a designer. We would advise them to take the less-expensive option, even though we will make a little less money.

As marketing experts, we share our knowledge with the talent we place. Our marketing talent know how to manage their resources well. They learn better processes, make better use of the people they have, make better use of technology.

Erin sees the bond that talent develops with Aquent as critical to their effectiveness working for Aquent's customers. This means offering competitive pay and benefits to talent, and the best staffing firms are going well beyond that to become employers of choice to talent they place. To this end, she says, "I develop programs that are going to attract and retain the best talent in the market. We have lots of conversations about work/life fit and we offer good pay and all kinds of benefits, but the big value is that we understand them, we know where they will succeed, and we seek to make a great match with a client."

John Wilson, who runs staffing firm Wilson Recruiting, treats the talent he represents exactly as a strong organization would treat full-time employees. "Wherever they work, we offer our people benefits that coincide exactly with the employer. For example, if a company's using a Fidelity 401(k) plan and we've placed contractors there, we make sure they have a Fidelity 401(k). If they're using UnitedHealthcare, we would make sure that we would have the exact same plan that they would have as full-time employees. As a result, the contractors we place in a company don't feel they're getting a deal that's any different from the full-time employees there. And our retention rate—the contractors who choose to stay with Wilson Recruiting—has been phenomenal."

Staffing companies who apply these strategic practices as intermediaries between client and talent have an increasingly important role to play in the

MY POV

"A good relationship between a staffing professional and an employer client is so much more than presenting a résumé and asking, 'Does this meet your requirements?' We work to understand both the client perspective and the candidate perspective in order to make that good fit. It starts with a deep understanding of your client's business and culture. Then we have a qualitative conversation with candidates about their experience, background, and overall arc of their careers, so that we can place them at the right clients, doing the right kind of work. Many times an employer client has said, 'Maybe this candidate didn't have exactly the skills that we're looking for, but they were such a perfect fit from the culture perspective that they worked out great.' "

—*Erin Bloom, Director of Marketing for Talent, Aquent*

decentralized, project-based practices of today's business. Those who stay with the old transactional model will struggle to find talent and satisfy their customers, but those who embrace and lead the changes will thrive.

Boomerang Employees

They once worked in your organization, and now they're back for a second term. Some left thinking the grass was greener elsewhere (and maybe it was!) Some were lost in layoffs or departed to return to school. A couple of decades ago, they might have been regarded as disloyal, or a bad risk, but the breakdown of the old employment contract has made that issue irrelevant. They have the skills you need, and they know a lot about your culture, and they even have a hard-eyed understanding of the world "out there," where the grass isn't necessarily greener. No matter—boomerang employees can bring great value back to the company. Their onboarding time is shorter; they have established relationships; they have gained knowledge and experience that profits the organization today. You can also hire them with relative ease, and if you have kept an institutional memory, you have an accurate idea of what they will deliver.

The key to attracting boomerang employees is to maintain a connection with those who leave. Earlier, we mentioned alumni newsletters or mailing lists for those who depart, and yours should contain nonconfidential company news and an updated list of open positions. You can ask people to join the mailing list (at a personal e-mail address) when they leave. You might find that many are reluctant, especially if they're being laid off. If a good employee declines, ask if you can follow up in six months.

Remember, too, that even if a good employee never becomes a boomerang hire, he might become a valuable networking resource. Don't let him get away! Also, it's smart to quietly triage employees into those who you would have back, those who you'd like to keep an eye on, and those whose departure was a relief (abusive or incompetent people, for example). Make a note when you close their files—or better yet, keep a separate list of people you'd like to rehire. They are a strong component of a recruiter or manager's network. (And who knows where you'll both be seven years from now?)

Community

The sixth trend, community, keeps reappearing in new forms online. Twenty years ago it was the lively conversation on crude electronic bulletin boards. Ten years ago it was evident in heavy message board postings at sites like Yahoo! The rise of social networking is just the newest manifestation of an ancient truth: people want to connect with like-minded people. From the agora of Athens to LinkedIn.com, community appears in any venue it can.

Community is and will be a huge asset for the relationship-minded employer. People inside and outside the company discuss your organization through all their roles in the Engagement Cycle. Soon, prospective candidates will join a long-term conversation about your organization, seeking out trustworthy connections and forming their own views. When their peers validate your employer branding efforts, candidates will listen. The topic is nothing new: what do people talk about at college, fraternity, and company reunions besides work? What's new, and growing, is the seamless and ongoing nature of the conversation.

Social networking services, as discussed in Chapter 7, are not fully satisfactory yet, but they have come a long way in the last couple of years. What's emerging is an intriguing combination of media vehicles and social connection software that forms communities of interest around information. How that will make the leap into genuine relationships between you and the most promising candidates has yet to be seen, but it's beginning to happen, so embrace these technologies. Get online and experience them. When it happens, what will matter is the power and authenticity of your employer brand.

Everyone's an Evangelist

Community includes the people who might work at your company, who work at your company today, and who once worked at your company. What do they believe, in their hearts, is your employer brand?

An employee referral program will provide incentive for your current staff to bring in talent, but companies that really keep their pipeline filled train their employees to promote their employer brand with the enthusiasm of a true evangelist. That goes for executives as well as entry-level employees. In a time when 70 percent of employees are poised to move for a better offer, why not reinforce the best reasons to stay with the team?

Teach your recruiting message to your employees. Have them repeat it. Reward them for learning it. Throw parties and ask them to invite their friends, just to take a look, just to spread the word. Get your recruiters to have lunch with your executives, and vice versa. Everyone recruits, and everyone's on the lookout for talent. Relating to poised workers, active candidates and each other throughout the Engagement Cycle, living your employer brand, everyone working at your organization becomes an evangelist.

Review

- In the coming years, next practices in hiring will be driven by accelerating changes in transparency, interactivity, mobility, diversity, flexibility, and community.
- Next practices open new channels to reach candidates, and to engage your employer brand with new audiences.
- Effective hiring of new resources requires you to rethink more than outreach. Work arrangements themselves might change.
- Staffing organizations can capitalize on shortages by guiding clients to new ways of working.
- Talent shortages will increase the value of boomerang employees, unorthodox search methods, and outreach.
- Everyone in a strongly branded employer must be an evangelist for talent and be rewarded for finding keepers.

Afterword

The new relationship among employers, employees, and candidates will determine whether organizations succeed or fail in the coming decade. Its context is the talent tsunami sweeping through the world of business, and its operating principle is the Engagement Cycle.

In the last 20 years, employers regarded employees as assets, not as a community, and that behavior created a consumer mindset among candidates and employees alike. That's why 70 percent of employees are poised, open to new opportunity. Economic, social, and technological factors have empowered poised workers, and they are not going back to the old deal.

All the measures that we have described, from building a good employer brand, to focusing on intangible benefits, to devoting attention to your best players, to treating candidates with the respect each deserves, reveal a different attitude. You can change the rules of a very old game by moving away from transactional hiring and moving toward relationship building around a strong and authentic employer brand. If you treat people the way they want to be treated, offer the right things fairly, and strive to follow a set of values in your workplace, you'll get the right people on board.

We've got plenty of examples around the world of companies that have very low turnover, in industries that are straining to find enough talented workers. Their strength didn't happen by accident. People from full-time recruiters to executive leadership to line managers learned to attract, acquire, and advance the smart and capable workers they needed. They treat those people well. Day by day they manage relationships with workers characterized by mutual respect, shared values, and authenticity. It's not easy work, but the results are worth the effort.

It comes down to this: do you treat people as human beings or do you treat them as assets, as commodities? If you don't care about people, they'll have a hard time caring about you. But if you care about them as employees, as friends, as partners in business, and as neighbors and colleagues, they're bound to join you and stay engaged. Respect, recognition, and engagement are the essence of finding keepers.

Resources

Online Resources

Bizstats

www.bizstats.com
"No chat, just stats." A broad resource for U.S. business statistics, especially small business.

The Bureau of Labor Statistics
www.bls.gov

The Economist online (world section)
http://www.economist.com/world/
Superb reporting on world business. Country briefings at www.economist.com/countries/ contain excellent information on employment and economic trends in more than 80 countries.

Electronic Recruiting Exchange (ERE)
www.ere.net
One of the most prolific and broad-reaching resources for hiring expertise. The Electronic Recruiting Exchange's daily columns are informative, entertaining, and relevant to anyone who hires. ERE also runs human-resources expos.

Eurostat

http://epp.eurostat.ec.europa.eu/

The Statistical Office of the European Communities publishes extensive labor market information across the European markets.

Human Capital Institute

www.humancapitalinstitute.org

A member organization, think tank, and educational resource for human capital professionals.

Interbiznet

www.interbiznet.com

Interbiznet is an online guide to and critique of recruiting. Founder John Sumser is particularly insightful about hiring technology and strategic recruiting. His *Electronic Recruiting News* e-mail newsletter is a must-read for industry insiders.

Monster Intelligence

http://intelligence.monster.com

Monster Intelligence is the research division of Monster.com. At this site, you'll find in-depth reports on dozens of topics in hiring and managing today's skilled workers. Many of these reports formed the research background of *Finding Keepers*, and they will be updated over time. You'll also find free webinars on subjects like high-volume hiring, employer branding, benefits, worker engagement, and finding top talent. Many reports and webinars are produced in cooperation with other human capital leaders such as the Human Capital Institute and DDI, Inc.

http://hiring.monster.com

This is the section of Monster.com dedicated exclusively to employers.

National Human Resource Association

www.humanresources.org

A U.S. association of affiliate member groups promoting human resources practices.

The Occupational Outlook Handbook

www.bls.gov/oco

Two sites from the U.S. Department of Labor contain a wide variety of advice, information, and statistics, including excellent job descriptions and data on U.S. labor supply and demand trends. Non-U.S. labor statistics can be found at www.bls.gov/fls/.

Society for Human Resource Management (SHRM)

www.shrm.org

The Society for Human Resource Management (SHRM) is the world's largest organization devoted to human resource management, with members in more than 100 countries. Its Web site has abundant information, resources, and research (some resources are available to members only). SHRM also publishes HR *Magazine* for human resource professionals.

The Wall Street Journal Online

www.wsj.com (membership required)

Excellent Asian and European sections with original reporting and data.

Workforce Management

http://workforce.com

Includes content from *Workforce Management* magazine, research, and several helpful e-mail newsletters.

Books

The following books are not all focused exclusively on hiring but speak well to the issues raised in *Finding Keepers*.

Buckingham, Marcus, and Curt Coffman. *First, Break All the Rules: What the World's Greatest Managers Do Differently*. New York: Simon & Schuster, 1999.

Cappelli, Peter. *The New Deal at Work*. Boston: Harvard Business School Press, 1999.

Collins, Jim. *Good to Great*. New York: Harper Business, 2001.

Fisher, Roger, Richard Ury, and Bruce Patton. *Getting to Yes: Negotiating Agreement Without Giving In*, 2nd Ed. Boston: Houghton Mifflin 1992.

Fitz-Enz, Jac. *How to Measure Human Resources Management*, 3rd Ed. New York: McGraw-Hill, 2001.

Huselid, Mark, Brian Becker, and Richard Beatty. *The Workforce Scorecard*. Boston: Harvard Business School Press, 2005.

Kaye, Beverly, and Sharon Jordan-Evans. *Love 'em or Lose 'em: Getting Good People to Stay*. San Francisco: Barrett-Koehler Publishers, Inc., 1999. Beverly Kaye is Founder and CEO of Career Systems International, www.careersystems intl.com. Sharon Jordan-Evans is President of the Jordan Evans Group, www.jeg.com.

Losey, Mike, Sue Meisinger, and Dave Ulrich, eds. *The Future of Human Resource Management*. Hoboken, NJ: John Wiley & Sons, 2005.

Martin, Carole. *Boost Your Hiring IQ*. New York: McGraw-Hill, 2007.

Michaels, Ed, Helen Handfield-Jones, and Beth Axelrod (McKinsey & Co.). *The War for Talent*. Boston: Harvard Business School Press, 2001.

Taylor, Jeff, and Doug Hardy. *Monster Careers: Networking*. New York: Penguin, 2005.

Taylor, Jeff, and Doug Hardy. *Monster Careers: Interviewing*. New York: Penguin, 2006.

Notes

Chapter 1

1. From Monster research. Total costs also include human resource and recruiting staff, technology, management time, retention costs, hiring bonuses, and other costs directly related to hiring and retaining skilled employees.
2. Michael Pilot, BLS Monthly Labor Review, February, 2004. More interpretation in Robert J. Grossman's "The Truth about the Coming Labor Shortage," HR Magazine, Volume 50, No. 3, March 2005.
3. National Science Board, Science and Engineering Indicators 2004, National Science Foundation, Division of Science Resources Statistics, Arlington, VA (NSB 04-01), May 2004.
4. McKinsey & Co., "The Emerging Global Labor Market, Part II," June 2005.
5. Michael W. Horrigan, "Employment Projections to 2012. Concepts and Context," BLS Monthly Labor Review, February 2004, p. 14.
6. "Many qualified applicants are being turned away because of a shortage of nursing faculty to teach classes," BLS OOH 2006-7. http://www.bls.gov/oco/ocos083.htm#outlook. Accessed September11, 2007.
7. "Utilities Brace for Worker Shortage," USA Today, May 16, 2007, http://www.usatoday.com/money/economy/employment/2007-05-16-power-shortage-cover_n.htm.
8. Congress reduced the number of American H1B visas ("the high-tech worker visa") from 215,000 before September 11, 2001 to 66,000, and that limit remains in place today (the demand is easily three to five times that number).
9. The New Yorker, April 30, 2007.
10. "China's Looming Human Talent Shortage" by Diana Farrell and Andrew J. Grant – McKinsey Quarterly, 2005 No. 4.
11. James Surowiecki, "It's the Workforce, Stupid!" The New Yorker, April 30, 2007. Said Surowiecki: "Too many companies today define workers solely in terms of how much they cost, rather than how much value they create. . . . After downsizing, it's easier to measure a lower wage bill than it is to see the business the company isn't getting because it has too few salesmen, or the new products it isn't inventing because its R. & D. staff is too small."

12. Baruch Lev of New York University's Stern School of Business is the leader in this field. Citations include *The Economist* and ITWorld.com.
13. According to the Bureau of Labor Statistics, employment rose about 12 percent and wages increased 5 to 6 percent.

Chapter 2

1. "Your Loyal Workers and How to Keep Them That Way," Monster Intelligence, Fall 2006, see http://intelligence.monster.com/11448_en-US_p1.asp.
2. From Monster/DDI selection forecast, "Slugging Through the War for Talent," June 2007, see http://intelligence.monster.com/12338_en-US_p1.asp.
3. "Slugging Through the War for Talent."
4. "A Changing Landscape, The Effect of Age, Gender and Ethnicity on Career Decisions," (webinar) Monster Diversity and Inclusion, http://intelligence.monster.com/10792_en-US_p1.asp.
5. "A Changing Landscape." This factor is important to 46 percent of those ages 50 and above, compared to 39 percent of those ages 35 to 49, and 27 percent of those ages 18 to 34.
6. "Benefits of the Future: Employer Perspective," Monster Intelligence, 2006, http://intelligence.monster.com/11768_en-US_p1.asp.

Chapter 3

1. Not-for-profit organizations achieve greater advancement of their mission.
2. Peter F. Drucker, *The Essential Drucker*, New York: HarperCollins, 2003.

Chapter 4

1. As *Finding Keepers* went to press, Dan Hilbert (with the backing of venture capitalists) formed Orca Eyes, Inc., a strategic workforce performance optimization software and consulting services company.
2. Many models for this are available at all levels of complexity. The Conference Board's Working Group on Evidence-Based Human Resources, Kenexa Workforce Intelligence, and the Society for Human Resource Management are good sources for finding the latest information in modeling. Monster Intelligence also includes information on this topic on its Web site: http://intelligence.monster.com.

Chapter 5

1. "Employer Branding Survey 2003," The Economist/TMP Worldwide, May 2003. Presentation, slide 17.
2. From the Great Place to Work Institute, "Best Small and Medium Companies to Work for in America." http://www.greatplacetowork.com/best/list-sme-2007.htm.
3. See http://www.eileenfisher.com/.
4. See http://www.intuit.com/careers/culture.jhtml.

5. "Cisco's Connections," *U.S. News and World Report*, http://www.usnews.com/usnews/biztech/articles/060626/26best.htm (accessed June 26, 2006).

Chapter 6

1. "Using Branding to Attract Talent," *McKinsey Quarterly*, 2005, No. 3.

Chapter 7

1. It's not our purpose here to sell Internet recruiting but to describe it as a medium. Recruiters and hiring managers make strategy first and then decide on tactics such as which channels to use.
2. Monster Intelligence Survey, 2007.

Chapter 8

1. "Google Answer to Filling Jobs is an Algoithm," *New York Times*, Jan. 3, 2007.
2. *Monster Careers: Interviewing* contains over 500 different interview questions, with analysis and sample answers, as well as descriptions of the major interview styles.
3. An excellent source for this is the popular *How Would You Move Mt. Fuji?* by William Poundstone, New York: Little, Brown and Co., 2003.
4. ERE newsletter, February 19, 2007.

Chapter 9

1. Monster webinar, "The Five Stages of New Hire Orientation and On-boarding," November 2006. http://intelligence.monster.com/11128_en-US_p1.asp.
2. From Monster/DDI selection forecast, "Slugging Through the War for Talent," June 2007. http://intelligence.monster.com/12338_en-US_p1.asp.
3. "Slugging Through the War for Talent."
4. You can find a more detailed but still simple turnover cost calculator at the U.S. Department of Labor: www.dol.gov/cfbci/turnover.htm.
5. Yves Lermusiaux, *Strategic Talent Management: Calculating the High Cost of Employee Turnover*, 2007; http://www.taleo.com/research/articles/strategic/calculating-the-high-cost-employee-turnover-15.html (accessed May 4, 2007).
6. *Tug of War: Exploiting the Benefit Opportunity Gaps*, Monster Intelligence, Spring 2007.
7. *Tug of War*.
8. These HR managers say that a supervisor's poor retention grades can reduce the merit increase of a manager or result in a smaller bonus. In extreme cases, a manager's poor retention grades can be grounds for dismissal.
9. Monster Intelligence, "Retention Strategies for 2006 and Beyond," Winter 2006.
10. This and other data from Monster webinar, "The Five Stages of New Hire Orientation and On-boarding," November 2006. http://intelligence.monster.com/11128_en-US_p1.asp.

11. Trade union congress case study, 15 October 2005, http://www.tuc.org.uk/work_life/
    tuc-10980-f0.cfm; European Industrial Relations Observatory online:
    http://www.eurofound.europa.eu/eiro/2006/08/articles/it0608019i.html.

Chapter 10

1. Manpower, "Talent Shortage Survey 2007 Global Results," p.2.
2. "After Complaints, Dell to Stop Routing Support Calls to India" *Wall Street Journal*, November
   24, 2003. Also "New Economy; Companies Sending Work Abroad are Learning Cultural
   Sensitivity—to their American Customers," *New York Times*, December 8, 2003.

Chapter 11

1. "A Changing Landscape: The Effect of Race, Gender and Ethnicity on Career Decisions."
   Copyright Monster Diversity & Inclusion, 2006; also "Bridging the Gap: Diverse Job
   Seekers, Employers and the Internet" by Monster in association with Diversity Best
   Practices, Inc.
2. McKinsey & Co. "The Emerging Global Labor Market Part II—The Supply of Offshore Talent
   in Services," June 2005.

Index

About the Authors

Steve Pogorzelski

Steve Pogorzelski has held critical leadership positions at Monster for nine years. As Executive Vice President Global Sales & Customer Development, Steve is responsible for Monster sales and customer development in 40 countries. Prior positions at Monster have included President of Monster North America, where he was responsible for sales, marketing, customer service, and Monster Government Solutions. In addition, he was also responsible for other Monster properties in North America including FastWeb, Making It Count, MonsterTrak, and Military Advantage.

Pogorzelski brought over 16 years of recruitment advertising agency experience to Monster, encompassing a wide variety of functional areas. Prior to Monster, he was the Senior Vice President of Sales & Marketing for TMP Worldwide (now Monster Worldwide), the parent company of Monster. In that position, Pogorzelski was responsible for agency business development in nine countries on three continents. Pogorzelski joined Monster in December 1998, after working with TMP for seven years.

Pogorzelski is a graduate of the University of Wisconsin with a B.A. in Journalism/Advertising. He has 23 years of recruitment advertising agency experience encompassing a wide variety of functional areas. He is also a current board member of Management Leadership for Tomorrow, Goodwill Industries, Heart of a Champion, and a former member of the National Board of Directors for the Employment Management Association. Pogorzelski is a monthly guest on CNBC's *Squawk Box* and Bloomberg Television. He is frequently quoted in the national and local press on employment-related topics.

Jesse Harriott, Ph.D.

 Dr. Harriott is currently Vice President of Global Monster Insights. He built Monster Intelligence, the research division at Monster focused on the human capital marketplace and has grown the division into Global Monster Insights, the company's international research arm. Global Monster Insights provides groundbreaking information and custom market analysis to help Monster customers make informed decisions about today's most pressing human capital issues. Dr. Harriott also pioneered the creation of the Monster Employment Index, the first measure of online recruitment activity— now tracked in the United States and Europe and followed by millions of people each month, including many government agencies.

Before Monster, Dr. Harriott was the Director of Market Research & Consulting for Gomez, Inc. where he led divisions that accounted for 60 percent of the company's revenue. Prior to joining Gomez, Dr. Harriott was founder and President of IMA, Inc, a first-of-breed Internet research company, as well as the Director of Research Consulting for public relations firm Lipman Hearne. He has also taught Internet marketing and marketing research courses at the University of Chicago, National-Louis University, and DePaul University. Dr. Harriott holds an M.A. and a Ph.D. in Experimental Psychology from DePaul University. He has appeared in various media outlets including CNBC, *The Wall Street Journal*, *New York Times*, CBS radio, Bloomberg Television, and Reuters.

Doug Hardy

Doug Hardy was the Editor-in-Chief of Monster and currently runs Monster's publishing program for employers and job seekers. He is the coauthor, with Monster founder Jeff Taylor, of three books in the *Monster Careers* series. He is also the coauthor (with Mark Kantrowitz, of Monster subsidiary Fastweb.com) of *Fastweb College Gold*, a guide to student financial aid. A certified job and career transition coach, Hardy gives presentations and conducts workshops on career-related topics at such venues as The Omega Institute, private job seeker organizations, and colleges. He is interviewed on employment topics by newspapers, magazines, television, and radio outlets around the country. Recent appearances include: *The Washington Post*, *The New York Post*, *Boston.com*, *The Tucker Carlson Show*, and national radio networks.

Prior to joining Monster, Hardy directed book, magazine, and web publishing businesses in New York and Boston for such media companies as Random House, Inc., The New York Times Magazine Co., and AT&T New Media.